Lady Father

A HUMOROUS, HEART-FELT, AND EYE-OPENING NARRATIVE OF A MARRIAGE COMMISSIONER'S EXPERIENCES

Edna I. McCall

Regina, Saskatchewan, Canada

Copyright © Edna I. McCall, 2021

All rights reserved. No part of this book may be reproduced in any form without permission in writing from the author. Reviewers may quote brief passages in reviews.

Published 2021

DISCLAIMER

No part of this publication may be reproduced or transmitted in any form or by any means, mechanical or electronic, including photocopying or recording, or by any information storage and retrieval system, or transmitted by email without permission in writing from the author.

Neither the author nor the publisher assumes any responsibility for errors, omissions, or contrary interpretations of the subject matter herein. Any perceived slight of any individual or organization is purely unintentional.

Brand and product names are trademarks or registered trademarks of their respective owners.

Cover Design: Nakita Duncan

Editing: Hott + Hadley Writing Consultancy

Author Photo Credit: Instinct Photography

ADVANCE PRAISE

"This is not only a book about 'marriages,' but a personal life story of my beautiful friend Edna — filled with history, laughter, joy, and touching moments. There are so many unique wedding experiences to read in this book as well as personal touches and thoughts. You will want to read it again and again. What an inspirational book to always pursue your dreams at any age and always try new things. Happy reading."

— Bev Kirk, friend of Edna

"This is Edna's first authorship, but I assure you this is not her first attempt to communicate. This is displayed remarkably with her usual flair of imagination and unique sense of humor; you will find out why she was so successful in this second vocation. Unlike the traditional occasions, each of these events were orchestrated by her leaving everyone with more than just special memories and I assure you it was because no two events were the same. Enjoy and compare this storyteller's remarkable experiences for yourself. It's a hoot!"

— Roland C. Richardson, author and artist

"Edna's writing style is exactly what Edna is — humorous, witty, concise, and full of compassion. She is a natural storyteller, sharing the joys of dropping into people's lives during a momentous time in their life. Her loyalty to her profession is amazing, for better or for worse. I had many feelings and reactions while reading each chapter, the predominant ones being to laugh, lots of right-out-loud laughs, sometimes just a little chuckle, and of course, there were many, many smiley moments. Well done, my friend."

— Geri Colter, friend and kindred spirit

"The intro of *Lady Father* had me hooked. *Lady Father* paints a wonderful journey through so many happy moments that Edna was part of. I felt I was there in all of the weddings that Edna describes, the traditions that other cultures have, and Edna revealing her own culture with her family. With all the different types and locations of marriages, Edna never skipped a beat. Even having weddings in her house – that is dedication. Edna would have a thousand more she could think about and smile at."

— Lyle Fluter, friend of Edna

"A most enjoyable read. Edna demonstrates her passion and creativity while performing unique, diverse, meaningful marriage ceremonies. I especially found the multi-cultural traditions to be most interesting as well as the varied venues."

— Myrna Steer, friend of Edna

"After performing more than 2,000 marriage ceremonies, Edna has enough stories to capture your attention for hours. She shares some of the funny, bizarre, unique, unfortunate but most certainly memorable events that have happened over the years. Edna's youthful zest for life shines through with each story and a snippet from her past. From riding in on a Harley, marrying people in jail, performing in costume, falling flat on her face, to jumping into a wrestling ring – you never know what is going to happen on the next page!"

— Shauntel Lemon, granddaughter of the Lady Father

"A light-hearted and fascinating journey through love, marriages and life inspiration awaits. *Lady Father* is an enjoyable read that will motivate you to live your life to the fullest. Thank you for sharing your book. You are truly an inspiration."

— Cornelius W. V. Martens, principal,
Marwest Group of Companies

"At first glance of the book cover, I knew Edna must possess an adventurous zest for life. In reading *Lady Father*, I felt engaged and interested to learn more of the history, as well as the numerous memorable and amazing experiences in her life as a marriage commissioner. There are also candid and surprising stores that I could not have imagined. Edna's true compassion for all couples she performs marriage ceremonies for are felt throughout the book. I recommend *Lady Father* especially if you have had the pleasure of meeting Edna. You will feel all the emotions as I have."

— Pat Jacobson, cardiology technologist
and married by Edna

DEDICATION

For my late husband, Bob, who always supported me in any of the endeavors that I chose to undertake. When I promoted through the ranks in my workplace, he was so proud of me and always encouraged me along the way. He was the best caregiver one could wish for. When I was appointed marriage commissioner, we became a team. We were together and he patiently listened to more than 2,000 ceremonies that I performed.

For my late sister, Florence (Flo), who would have yelled from the rooftops, "Book for sale! Book for sale!" She was so proud when I was appointed marriage commissioner and was excited whenever she came to Regina and I needed a witness she would be a "bridesmaid," which was Flo's interpretation of a witness.

A gift from Irma, a dear friend, symbolizing love, marriage, and commitment.

CONTENTS

Foreword	1
Chapter 1: The Ride Begins	3
Chapter 2: Setting Things Straight	9
Chapter 3: Where It All Began	19
Chapter 4: Dearly Beloved	29
Chapter 5: I Promise to Accept You, Protect You, And Love You	41
Chapter 6: May My Arms Be Your Shelter and My Heart Be Your Home	55
Chapter 7: Honouring Cultures	59
Chapter 8: Going That Extra Mile	77
Chapter 9: Same-Sex Marriages	83
Chapter 10: Memorable Celebrations	93
Chapter 11: Oddball Weddings	107
Chapter 12: Biker Wedding	111
Chapter 13: Crashes and Falls	117
Chapter 14: The Darndest Places	123
Chapter 15: Wedding Party Bloopers	135
Chapter 16: How I Became Lady Father	143
Chapter 17: Truly Unique	149
Chapter 18: Till Death Do Us Part	155
Acknowledgments	159
About the Author	161

FOREWORD

Lady Father is a book documenting at least two things: it is the narrative of Edna's journey after retirement, using her extraordinary character to create a new career in life. And it shows how one woman proves her power to make a difference.

Just think about it: Edna combines social skills, love of acting, artistic eye, and organisational experience to create her very special take on the role of marriage commissioner. And she has performed more than 2,000 weddings! Almost all of those were with her late husband Bob as driver and assistant. Her stories show an incredible range of couples, settings, themes, situations; reading the table of contents makes you curious, as well as want to go back and read again after you close the last page. She is one tough Lady Father; she is compassionate and full of humour.

I have known Edna since she performed Michael's and my wedding in 2005. Our search for the right marriage commissioner included one particular wish: we have many friends in same-sex relationships, and it was important to us to find someone with the integrity we thought should go with the job. And there was Edna! We still have her speech in writing. It is meaningful to us and we quote her from time to time.

I was greatly honoured to be asked to write this foreword. To my fellow readers I can only say: enjoy!

EDNA I. MCCALL

— Kari Mitchell, writer, blogger, editor, and married by Edna

CHAPTER 1:
THE RIDE BEGINS

I never imagined myself riding into a wedding on a motorcycle but found myself behind the groom on a Harley Davidson as he drove me to the front of the venue to perform their marriage ceremony. As we approached, the audience jumped up and took pictures of our flamboyant entrance. Sitting behind the groom that day, I felt like an angel with my arms outstretched giggling with excitement.

My angelic moment soon turned to awkwardness as I struggled to dismount with some degree of grace. I didn't fall (that time) but I did manage to maintain my composure as I walked to the front of the venue with great dignity and looking professional.

Of all the ceremonies I have performed, I have found myself in the most peculiar, ordinary, and beautiful places. I have often participated in unique traditional ceremonies like the breaking of the glass, smoking grass, jumping of the broom, and also being directed to remove my shoes and do the service in bare feet.

I couldn't possibly share each of my favourite moments during my time as a marriage commissioner in one book. Throughout these pages, however, I will share with you a few of my favourites, and some of the most intriguing – from riding on the back of a motorcycle, marrying the same people more than once, to the oddest places like the correctional centre. Being a marriage commissioner has been a wild ride so put your helmet on; you're going to need it.

When I retired from my long career at SGI, I contemplated what I would like to do next.

I felt disappointed but accepted the fact that there was a restricted age limit at sixty-five that forced me to retire. However, I had so much energy and wanted to keep contributing. There was no way that I was going to become a couch potato. But what to do? I wanted something involving people, something of a personal nature. I had always wanted to be a teacher but found that role fulfilled in my job at SGI as a supervisor and manager where I developed new staff when they came into my department.

I was looking for excitement, something that would give me a high and a sense of accomplishment. I loved acting and speaking in front of people. Soon after, to my delight, I attended my son Shawn's friend's wedding performed by a marriage commissioner. I was only used to religious church ceremonies and had heard that civil ceremonies were about five minutes long and contained legal information only. To me, legal was cold. To my surprise, that ceremony was extremely personal, containing beautifully written words that seemed to capture the real meaning of a marriage ceremony. She was about halfway through this beautiful service when I had a "wow" moment.

I decided being a marriage commissioner was what I wanted to do. I nudged my daughter-in-law, Rosanne, beside me and within a second, she said, "You want to do that?"

I said, "Yes, yes, yes!"

"Go for it," she said. "You will be good at it."

Upon inquiring, I was advised that the waiting period to begin would be five years which was fine as I could still work for four more years. However, in fifteen months, I received notification of my appointment from the Department of Justice which totally caught me off guard. I had received a substantial promotion at work within this time and did not want to resign.

I decided that I could handle both my day job and my appointment since the kids had left home and my husband, Bob, and I were on our own. Bob had retired from his job as a transit operator and was a full-time housekeeper, cook, grocery shopper, and gardener. I had the time to handle the extra work involved. I was one of six marriage commissioners in Regina and the surrounding area.

The first thing I did was contact my colleagues and get to know them to find out the process since there was no training. With great anticipation, I called the first marriage commissioner and introduced myself.

Was that ever a big mistake. She went cold as ice on me and just answered yes or no, contributing nothing to our conversation but silence. Since I was not getting anything but embarrassing silence, I thought I better end our conversation before she hangs up on me. I assumed she thought I would be a competitor instead of a colleague. Undaunted, I called another marriage commissioner since I thought, *They all can't be like that.*

Well, I struck gold the next time. She was friendly, congratulated me on my appointment, and asked if there was anything she could help me with. After having a conversation for about fifteen minutes, she suggested that we meet somewhere for coffee. I was elated to think that it was all going to work out. We had a wonderful conversation over coffee, and she gave me insight toward some of the dos and don'ts of performing a marriage ceremony. She was most helpful and over the years we became good friends. Any time I was in doubt about anything I would call her, and, in turn, she would have unique situations she would run by me.

I looked into what I would say during my charge to the couple. I went to the library to research civil ceremonies and I found that everything I looked at was antiquated and obsolete – not what I was looking for. The one thing that I didn't want to happen was that the couple would be disappointed with my mundane service as I felt with my ceremony years earlier. There was a wedding a week before ours and the couple wanted a basic, short ceremony with no vows – just "I do." Bob and I, on the other hand, wanted wedding vows and a lengthier service. We got the same short, basic service. When we got in the car, the first thing we said to each other was, "What about our vows?" We were both so disappointed.

I thought, *Hey, I can do this.* I decided to author in my words what I would say to the couple with the idea as to what I would like to hear.

My next project was to come up with a motto – "professional services with a personal touch," keeping in mind I wanted it to be professional and personal, as well. With that in mind, I designed and ordered my first set of business cards.

During my excitement, I never noticed that Bob was sitting in the background not knowing what to expect. He made a comment about me for sure never being home now. It was time to have a conversation about how we were going to handle this newfound situation. The weddings were held mostly on Saturdays, but sometimes Fridays and Sundays. We were okay with committing our weekends to the weddings since we decided that we would work together as a team. His responsibilities were to drive, find the address of the venue prior to leaving home, and not ask me how to get there on the way to the wedding. That would be a sure way to get me riled up before the ceremony. He would be responsible for the camera and take pictures of every couple and wedding party, and to look after my robe.

We were perfect partners. He did his homework exceptionally well. We got lost only once. He forgot the robe only twice. Luckily, we were always early which allowed us to get back and pick up the robe.

Upon arrival at the venue, where the weddings took place, I would go directly to do last minute instruction with the wedding party.

It bothered him and he felt conspicuous to walk into a venue with all strangers, especially small, intimate family weddings where everyone knew each other. Often, people would ask who he was or why was he there.

Eventually he got used to it and looked forward to *our* weddings. Ultimately this became our social life. That certainly kept him out of the easy chair where he was starting to spend more and more time.

I enjoyed my meetings with the couples, planning the wedding and setting the stage for my ceremonies. I could read immediately if the groom was not interested in participating in the process. The bride was always excited and gave me all the details. Then I thought, *Okay, I will warm him up*. I would ask him questions about what his thoughts were and after some coaching he would open up. Mostly, the guys would be so nervous and didn't know what to say. Surprisingly, I would get them talking and have an enjoyable time in our meetings. Often after the business part was over, we would sit and they would tell me about their life stories.

As they were leaving, I would give them a hug. They would walk out of my house all excited knowing what to expect, which was much more than they had anticipated.

From the beginning, I found myself emotionally involved with each couple I united. On occasion, I have asked several members of my family to act as witnesses and they, too, became emotionally bonded to these strangers.

Most couples remember that their objective is to enjoy their days to the fullest. The brides have been radiant, whether they wore a long, white gown with a train and headpiece or a turtleneck sweater with blue jeans.

Even in my professional role, I sometimes find it difficult to maintain my composure when two people are crying with joy and happiness directly in front of me. I learned before too long not to look at the bride's mother since, in a lot of cases, she was emotional.

I am not alone in my nostalgia. A wedding is such a beautiful, emotional event that you never know how a couple, their family, or guests will react. I have had a big, husky best man sob; he even used up my supply of tissues that I usually save for the bride and groom, bridesmaids giggling nervously, parents crying with happiness and relief, or unpredictable behavior from the flower girls and ring bearers.

The weddings increased tremendously in 1999 and 2000 as couples wanted to get married in the last year of the century and also during the millennium year.

I did weddings in combination with a nun, several alternative ministers, family members, or friends of the couple, Minister of the Seventh Day Adventist Church, a Catholic priest, and a pujari.

A wedding only represents the first hours of a marriage that is meant to be a lifetime commitment. But it is an important step in the crystallization of a romance. Judging by the increase in the number of marriages in recent years, romance is alive and well.

CHAPTER 2:
SETTING THINGS STRAIGHT

I would like to share a few tidbits on what a marriage commissioner is and how their duties differ from that of a clergy or justice of the peace. In 1972, Bob and I were asked to be the witnesses for my aunt's marriage ceremony at the courthouse. At 10:00 a.m. on a Tuesday morning, we entered the courthouse and were asked to take a seat while we waited for the justice of the peace (also referred to as a JP) to arrive. I was taken aback when he entered the room with his shirt button open leaving his hairy belly button exposed. He hardly looked up. He asked us to rise and spoke in a monotone and gruff voice. In my mind I was thinking this guy just didn't want to be there, and in no time at all, it was over. Done. From that experience and much to my delight, justices of the peace can no longer perform marriage ceremonies in the courthouse.

A justice of the peace may perform marriage ceremonies only if they hold a marriage commissioner appointment.

It was around 1980 that the marriage duties were separated from the justice of the peace duties; marriage commissioners were appointed and their sole function was to perform marriage ceremonies anywhere. Marriage commissioners are not allowed to use any religious connotations. It was difficult for me to imagine performing a marriage ceremony without reference to God. Up until that point, I had only ever attended religious ceremonies in churches. In a church ceremony, the officiant would talk about the love of God and how the couple would come together as one with God in their lives. The charge to the couple is all about the biblical interpretation that that particular church believed. There was also the restriction of the type of ceremony that would be performed and where the ceremony would be performed. For example, in some churches, a full mass is performed, which is not necessarily the wishes of the couple who are getting married – but they are not given an option in the church.

I knew that I had it in me to deliver a personal and meaningful ceremony that was full of the depth of love that the couple have for one another and that focused on the couple's commitment to each other. As a marriage commissioner, I give the couple choices and options of the type of ceremony they would like to have and the personal vows they wish to share with one another. They also get to choose where they get married. Rather than feeling restricted and having to follow a particular religious tradition, I now saw how I could infuse the spirit of God's love in my ceremonies by speaking to a much broader interpretation of God's love that included the marriage of any sexual orientation, culture, tradition, or faith. The sky was the limit. I worked hard to create a meaningful and loving service that was fulfilling to me. I know I was successful in doing this as I have been told many times how happy and delighted the couple were with my ceremony. They would say, "Our guests would come up to us and say how beautiful the service was."

Here is an example of the attitude of a person coming to a ceremony performed by a marriage commissioner. The wedding was held at the Double Tree Hotel with 200 invited guests. One of the guests was overheard telling her friend, "I don't know why I came for the ceremony since they are having a JP and they are usually a five-minute thing, but I thought it wouldn't look too good walking in after the ceremony just for the reception." I had put a lot of work into this ceremony since the bride was a lawyer and the groom a principal, and they knew what they wanted their ceremony to look like. My service was over a half hour. I did a beautiful reading entitled "These Hands," and also performed the rose ceremony where I had the mothers of the bride and groom present roses to their son and daughter. I then proceeded by saying, "In the elegant language of flowers, red roses are a symbol of love, and the giving of a single red rose is a clear and unmistakable way of saying the words, 'I love you.' For this reason, it is fitting that the first gift you exchange as husband and wife be the gift of a single red rose."

The bride and groom exchanged roses and said, "I love you" to each other.

I continued with, "In the best of marriages there are difficult times. There are times of hurtful words, times of neglect, times when we must patiently wait to be together again. Those may be times when the words you need to speak are difficult. I ask that you remember this moment and that when words fail you, you place a single rose on your spouse's pillow as a way to say, 'I love you.' Let this exchanging of roses be the beginning of a lifelong tradition of unspoken love."

I felt on top of my game with this performance. The woman was eating her words after the ceremony when everyone was complimenting me on my service on the way out.

This woman was not the only person I came across with a negative attitude toward marriage commissioners. A bride's grandmother who came from Ontario for the wedding came up to me after the service and said, "I am a staunch Roman Catholic and I have never been to a wedding with a JP before, but did I ever enjoy your service." Throughout the reception she repeated the same story several times. The grandfather came up to me and said, "That was good. You sure told them what they needed to hear."

Another bride had two aunts who came all the way from Ottawa, Ontario. They were not pleased that their niece was getting married in their backyard by a JP, no less. Being staunch Anglican, they wanted nothing more than an Anglican church wedding. After the ceremony one of the aunts rushed up to me and said, "We wanted you to know that we disagreed with our niece to be married by a JP in her backyard, but you were as close to the church as you can get," as she tweaked my cheek. "Beautifully done. I am pleased that we came despite our objections."

Some of the reasons couples may choose to have civil ceremonies is because they each have different religious beliefs, no affiliation to any church, or are divorced and unable to marry in their church. My son, Shawn, asked me what the common denominator is for the reason why people choose a marriage commissioner. My answer to him was religious beliefs. You couldn't get married in the Catholic Church if you were divorced, if you were living together, or if you had children.

However, in a lot of cases, it is because the couple would like something unique and different, and they would like to customize their ceremony and structure their vows, as well as decide where they would like to hold it. One of my favorite parts of being a marriage commissioner is customizing the ceremonies to the couples wishes. Of course, I would also add my condiments to the pot from the stories they shared with me. I would often get a chuckle from the crowd. There were also times that I was the brunt of the joke, like the time the father of the bride rushed up to where I was standing at the close of the ceremony and presented me with a huge bag of sunflower seeds. This was payback from when he would spit those seeds all over our kitchen floor back in our youth, and thoroughly annoyed us to the point we would kick him out of the house, only to have him return the next evening. I was shocked that he remembered but enjoyed his sense of humor. Incidentally,

I accepted the sunflower seeds.

You do not have to be a Saskatchewan resident in order to be married here, but the marriage license must be a Saskatchewan license. I had the privilege of marrying a couple who drove all the way from Louisiana to be married in Regina, Saskatchewan, because they could not be married in their state.

The age of majority in Saskatchewan is eighteen; anyone getting married under the age of eighteen must first obtain the consent of both parents. Your local marriage license issuer has the required consent forms.

I made an appointment to meet with a young couple for the interview at their place since they did not have a vehicle. After our usual small talk, I asked for their marriage license. Along with the marriage license, I was handed another document – a permission to marry form signed by the parents. I looked at the bride and asked how old she was. Twenty-one, she said. Then I asked the groom how old he was. Seventeen years of age, he said. I was shocked since the bride looked much younger than twenty-one – more like seventeen – and the groom looked more like twenty-one. I wondered if he might be too young to take such a serious, lifelong step. However, his parents agreed and signed the document, so I had no choice but to perform their marriage.

One of the things I enjoyed were the various venues that people chose to have their weddings. My most favorite place contained many unique trees and beautiful smelling flowers which changed with the seasons.

I was appointed a marriage commissioner on October 27, 1995. My first wedding was on December 16, 1995, in The City of Regina Greenhouse, now known as The Regina Floral Conservatory. I had never been there before but heard about it. I was in awe with what I saw when I entered the greenhouse for the first time. After my first wedding I was immediately smitten. When asked if I knew of a smaller venue, I would encourage couples to have their wedding at The City of Regina Greenhouse. I truly enjoyed performing weddings there since it was such a unique venue with the most gorgeous flowers and trees. I got attached to this place and decided when I retired from my job, I would volunteer there.

After my retirement I got in touch with the Regina Garden Associates, a non-profit organization who maintained the Floral Conservatory in 1999, I was sure that I did not want to get involved with any more meetings, become a board member, or be involved in anything with responsibilities. I had just recently retired and had enough meetings, decisions, and work. I wanted to do what I wanted to do. I just wanted to dig in the dirt and that is where I started in the display area on Tuesday mornings happily digging in the dirt.

In the meantime, I had a hard time convincing the couples that they were not getting married between the tomatoes and cucumbers when promoting The City of Regina Greenhouse. They did not want to send out wedding invitations naming the venue as a greenhouse.

My volunteer team would talk about the monthly meetings and the interesting guest speakers that they would have. I decided to attend the meetings and enjoyed the speakers, but I couldn't keep my mouth shut.

It was at one of these meetings when I mentioned my problem in convincing couples to have their weddings in a greenhouse and suggested a name change. I did not expect the response that I received. Some members were against a name change of any kind. Undaunted at the next monthly meeting, I asked if anymore thought was given to a name change. The president of the day said, "No," and moved on with other business.

The third month I thought, *I am going to keep at it until something is done,* so I mentioned this issue regarding a name change again and the president realizing I wasn't going to leave it alone said, "Do you want to go on the committee?" I said, "Absolutely." He asked for two more members in order to form a committee of three to come up with a name change.

The three committee members met shortly thereafter and discussed what approach to use to come up with a new name that would be suitable and more conducive to what that place was about. Each person took a different area to research and came back in a couple of weeks' time with their recommendations.

Within a month, we had a name to take to the meeting for approval. It was approved by the majority, however, not everyone was happy that the name should be changed at all.

The City of Regina did not take long to approve the name change. In fact, they were happy. Pat Fiacco, the mayor of Regina at that time, said, "Now that we have a professional name, we can advertise The Regina Floral Conservatory in the City of Regina tour guide, and they have every year since.

I volunteered in display from 1999 until 2007. I anxiously looked forward to Tuesday mornings when I could go to the Floral Conservatory and spend time in the serenity and peacefulness of the space. I enjoyed the watering and dead heading of the beautiful flower beds with the Tuesday team. Each team would pick a season that they would be responsible for. There were six season changes a year. Our team would discuss which season we wanted to do and start planning what flowers we would order, and basically took complete ownership of that season we chose. The first time I was so excited, and yet apprehensive as to where to start. Our leader asked another volunteer and I to take a bed and select what flowers we would use to design the bed. We asked her how we were to start, and she said, "That's up to you. Figure it out." We slowly started, and when it was done I was so excited to think that we did a great job in creating that beautiful bed.

Eventually, sadly, I had to quit since I had serious back issues from leaning over the flower beds.

I still wanted to be part of this beautiful space, so I started volunteering at reception on Wednesday afternoons with my friend Geri in the fall of 2007 and stayed for eight years.

During that time, I couldn't keep my mouth shut again, and became the reception coordinator from 2011 to 2014. I had to ensure there was always someone at reception every afternoon, seven days a week, and generally kept things going.

There were no policies and procedures when I started. I wrote policies and procedures for reception area and events committee. I worked with another volunteer to write procedures for other areas including rental and display communication. In 2003, the president of the day pursued me for several months to become the events coordinator. I finally agreed and continued in that capacity until 2019. I selected four members to be on my committee. Teas were our main focus. We established five teas per year. We immediately organized a structured tea schedule with times and ticket sales for each sitting. We also put a call out for china cups and saucers to replace Styrofoam cups. We recruited local musical performers ranging from country to pop to classical, instrumentals, and harpists. Just prior to each tea, we sent an email for volunteers to assist with each area on tea day. We required forty volunteers in all. We have been consistently sold out the last few years. On every tea day I would be on a real high to ensure everything would go well and for the most part it did. At the end of the day, I would feel such a sense of accomplishment and I would say, "Our committee is like a finely oiled machine. Everyone knew what they had to do and carried out their responsibilities as if their life depended on it." I also organized special events and volunteer appreciation events. So much for not wanting to get involved.

I was spending so much time at the floral conservatory that Bob often said that he would set up a bed for me so I could sleep there.

Over the years weddings and teas have become a major source of income for the Regina Floral Conservatory.

On September 2019, I was the proud recipient of my lifetime achievement award.

Edna and Bob at a special Floral Conservatory Dinner

CHAPTER 3:
WHERE IT ALL BEGAN

I have married more than 2,000 men. I have also married more than 2,000 women. As a marriage commissioner I have performed more than 2,000 ceremonies and have found each one to be as unique as the couples themselves. It doesn't matter whether there were more than 350 invited guests with a bridal party of fifteen or just the witnesses and the bride and groom. Each ceremony has been special and meaningful in their own ways. Growing up, I never imagined I would end up as a marriage commissioner helping shepherd so much joy into this world. And with that thought, I will begin with my story from growing up on the farm to my work experiences and family life.

I was born in a stone house on a farm along with my three sisters. Mom and Dad had mixed farming which was a large dairy farm plus grain. At age six, I would milk one cow in the evening. At age seven I would milk one in the morning, and two in the evening. That increased as I grew older. My dad would call us every morning before he went out to the barn. My sister, Flo, would get up immediately, but I was determined to get a few more winks.

When the cows were in the barn and Flo and Mom would start milking, and I was a no-show, Dad would come in thumping loud as he went up the stairs. I knew he was not in a good mood. I would grab my clothes and whiz right by him through the yard and into the barn. Dad didn't know what hit him. He came to the barn to check if, in fact I was there. And of course, I was.

As we became teenagers, we took on more responsibilities on the farm since obtaining hired help became difficult. We started working in the field picking stones, stooking, and helping with the threshing.

We had a threshing machine with a crew of six teams that would fill their hay racks with stooks and bring them to the threshing machine to unload. When I was fourteen and Flo was fifteen, we asked our dad if we could drive a team. Dad's instructions were simple.

"You can try it. The first time you're late, you're fired."

Our neighbour was a field pitcher who would assist all the crew so that everyone would get their load to the threshing machine on time. He would come to the rescue and ensure we would never be late. We were stiff and sore with blisters on our hands but smiling. We never did get fired. To top it off, we got a glass of chokecherry wine that my mom made and served to the crew each night for supper.

Whenever I pulled water out of the well to fill the tank, to cool the milk in eight-gallon cans, I would repeatedly say, "I want to be a city slicker." Finally for my grade twelve, I did get my wish; I left the farm for the bright lights of the city and for further education and a job. I went to Balfour Technical School in an all-boys class. I was so shy and uncomfortable at first, but my teacher, Gord Curry, saw to it that I was looked after. The boys never did harass me. Wanting so badly to leave the farm, I looked forward to going home to the fresh air, spaciousness, and tranquility of the farm.

My first permanent job was with the Royal Bank of Canada in downtown Regina. My aunt, who also worked downtown, and I would walk to work and home every day. In due course, my boyfriend would pick us up every morning and drive us home after work. Auntie sure loved that.

One September evening in 1954, I was sitting in the car in front of our house with my boyfriend when a brand-new car drove up behind us with Flo and two fellows whom I did not know. I was curious as to who was in the car with her. My boyfriend was jealous and he made me promise that I would not go out with these guys who he assumed were waiting for me. Of course, I promised and went into the house. Flo immediately followed me in and tried to convince me to go out with her. I was adamant that I promised my boyfriend I would not go out with her and the fellows in the car.

Flo became persistent and said, "This could be a chance of your lifetime." What I didn't know was that my boyfriend did not trust Flo or me and spied on us, watching me get into the car with the two fellows. Both were bus drivers and one was Bob McCall. I was not impressed with "this chance of a lifetime" that evening, and told Flo that. The next morning, Auntie and I ended up walking all the way downtown to work from Victoria Avenue E., since my faithful ride never showed. He never called again, either. After two weeks of being dateless, and Bob calling every evening asking Flo to talk me into going out with him, she finally convinced me to accept his invitation to the movies.

About two weeks later, Flo and I went to the farm to assist my parents with harvesting. What I did not know was that Flo invited Bob out after he was done with his shift on Sunday afternoon. I was in the field with my dad when Bob arrived at the farm, and Flo hid his car behind the barn so I would not know that he was there. When I came in from the field all dirty from shoveling grain in the bin only to find my new boyfriend of two weeks sitting there, I was so embarrassed to have him see me like that and ticked at Flo for doing this behind my back. He did not seem deterred by that. Bob knew from the beginning that I was the girl that he wanted to marry. I on the other hand, took longer. As time went by and I got to know him better, I fell more in love with him each day.

In January 1955, Bob totally surprised me with a proposal and a beautiful diamond ring. Of course, I said, "Yes." We were married on June 11, 1955. The wedding reception was held in the old stone house on the home farm as per my parents' wishes. They sold the farm shortly thereafter.

This was the beginning of our married life and raising our family. When I got pregnant, I was still working at the Royal Bank. Maternity clothes were not allowed. Therefore, I used to go to the Army and Navy store and buy an outfit a size bigger each time just so I could work longer. There was no maternity leave either, so I had to quit.

We had our first baby boy, Roddy, with gorgeous red hair. People would always comment on his red hair and how cute he was. His response was, "me no cute." When Rod was one year old, I went to work at Federated Co-op for six years until I got pregnant again. There was starting to be talk about maternity leave, but not yet implemented. Therefore, I had to quit work again.

Our second son, Shawn, was born much to Rod's chagrin since he was no longer the centre of all the attention. Suddenly he was to be the big boy now according to my mom, my aunt, and my sister who babied him all this time as their precious little boy. Who knew that this baby boy would become such a sports enthusiast in a non-sports family? It started right from when he was two years old, he would play goalie with a wooden spoon and tennis ball while watching hockey on TV with his dad. As he was growing up, he continued to participate in all sports including coaching, but hockey and playing goalie was his thing. We went to a lot of tournaments on many weekends through those years. When I would go to work on Monday mornings, my coworkers would ask me how my weekend was. I would tell them that I had blisters on my butt from sitting in the rink all weekend.

Shawn was fifteen months old when I went back to

work this time at SGI and stayed until I retired in 1998. I started as a keypunch operator and worked my way up through the ranks to a senior manager when I retired.

One of my most notable achievements at SGI was when I was promoted to facilities management. The first thing my new boss asked me to be responsible for was the evacuation program for the SGI tower. I was to immediately develop policies and procedures and have an evacuation plan. I called the fire department and introduced myself to the fire marshal. There was a moment of silence, then he said, "This is the third call from SGI. Two other fellows over the past couple of years have already called and were gung-ho about the evacuation program, and nothing has been done so far. And now today I get another call from SGI and a woman yet."

I thought, *I'll show him "a woman yet" will get the job done.* When the first evacuation was successfully completed, the fire marshal looked at me and said, "Congratulations, you did it." I pulled it off. I was most thankful to my supportive new boss for letting me run with this project without interference. He gave me the instructions and guidance when asked but let me handle the project totally.

On my last day of work, there was a fire drill. I was ticked off when the alarm went off. I wasn't going to participate in that drill. I was busy packing up my belongings and all of the bouquet of flowers that were sent to me for my retirement and I thought what a horrible time to have a drill. I changed my tune when the fire marshal came up to me and said, "Edna, you need to get down to our meeting spot at the legion."

I sassed him back and said, "I am too busy right now. I am packing. It is my last day and I have a lot to do. Besides, the limousine is coming to pick me up in less than an hour and I need to be ready." He rolled his eyes at me and then, with a demanding voice, commanded, "Edna, for God sakes, the fire drill is in your honour. Get your ass down to the legion – now."

I was shocked, surprised, and touched that they would bestow such an honour on me.

I looked at him and said, "For me?"

I took off and ran down the ten flights of stairs in my high-heel shoes like a scared rabbit without falling. The fire marshal followed behind me – way behind me. I arrived at the legion at high speed and out of breath with the fire marshal trailing behind. It was touching to see the legion packed with the employees from SGI. In that moment, I was reminded of my first evacuation many years ago and the impact that I had made as a trailblazer. During most of my employment with SGI, I rode in a carpool for twenty-six years with pretty much the same people. Oh, did we solve the world's problems. We called it, "As the carpool turns."

Our carpool driver, Barry Tappin, would stop across the street just three houses from my place at precisely 7:23 a.m. not 7:25 or 7:20, but precisely 7:23 a.m. One Halloween night it rained and by the next morning it was black ice. I was running across the street in my high-heels when I slipped and fell backwards. I could see car lights coming toward me so I quickly got up and into the car.

They were so busy talking they did not notice that I had fallen. I was so annoyed as I whimpered all the way to work. When I got to my office, I saw a bump like an egg hanging on my elbow. I was in so much pain. A staff member heard me whimpering, came in, and immediately drove me to the hospital. I had smashed my right elbow. Would you believe that thirty years later I am walking with my friend, Bev Kirk, in the park as we regularly did and slipped on black ice once again and fell backward, smashing my right elbow? The ambulance was called that time. The surgeon told me the next time I fall to break something else since it was difficult to repair a repair.

Upon my retirement, my staff arranged a fantastic retirement event for me at Queensbury Downs. It turned out to be a roast. Several past presidents attended as well.

Since I was not exactly a person of few words, there were a lot of stories to tell. The six roasters had good memories. However, I had the last word.

Every speaker was alluding to a story about the difficulties I had with my zipper on the back of my dress while on a road trip with two gentlemen from the office. When it was my turn I clarified the story by telling them that the zipper on the back of my dress had gotten stuck halfway down. I couldn't get it up or down. I opened the drapes in my hotel room and watched for one of the fellows to come by. As I saw the first one coming, I opened the door and said, "Jon, can you please help me? My zipper on the back of my dress is stuck." Without hesitation, Jon came into my room and began the struggle of trying to get the zipper to move. The second fellow was walking past my room on his way to the café. He had a look of shock on his face as he saw Jon standing close behind me, with my dress half open and struggling with the zipper. He had no idea if he was struggling to get my dress back on or to get my dress off. He quickly turned away and took off to the café. My retirement was in 1998 during the time of the Bill Clinton escapades. I ended my story by repeating Bill Clinton's famous last words, "I did not have sexual relations with that man, Mr. Schubert." This brought the house down. It was on our way home from this road trip that Jon said to me, "I am going to be president of SGI someday." I said, "Dream on you whippersnapper." And with that, he mumbled, "Edna, when I become president, you will have to kiss my feet. Can you believe it, he ultimately became president of SGI. I didn't have to kiss his feet though since I was already retired. Thank goodness. During these years my family grew up got married and had children.

My son Rod, who is still employed with the Provincial Government, is married to Liz, now a retired nurse, they have three girls. As they became teenagers, Rod would say it was PMS week every week. The eldest being Laura (Quenton), Kirsten (Nathan), and Jaclyn (Regan). And they have four grandchildren, Kara, Cruz, Alexander, and Jace. My son Shawn is a retired principal and is now employed with Regina Trades and Skills as a Program Manager. He is married to Rosanne, a retired teacher, they have four children. Shauntel (Jason), Sarah (Kelly), Derrick (Leah), Bryce (Jocelyn), and their nine grandchildren: Elijah, Julia, Maike, Aubry, Declan, Lydia, Maren, Frey, and Rowe.

When Shawn convocated from University of Regina he immediately started teaching out of town. Suddenly the shock of becoming empty nesters hit hard. No Shawn, no phone calls all evening long, no friends dropping in all the time. We started traveling throughout the years, and we took numerous trips across Canada, to Mesa, Arizona, Bermuda, Dominican Republic, Mexico, Europe, and Hawaii. We also enjoyed four cruises. Those cruises were the cat's meow. I truly enjoyed everything about the cruise, from being able to unpack my clothes to going to a different place every day to having a beautiful dinner and entertainment every evening.

When at home, we enjoyed time with our grandchildren as they came along, and as mentioned, you can see there was quite a few of them.

I love going to Saskatoon to visit my grandchildren there. Bryce owns The Backyard and that is when Great-Gramma becomes a child.

As well as being a scenario actor at RCMP Depot, I acted in the Tommy Douglas movie. I was dressed like a Hutterite woman and looked like one, too. I acted in seven episodes in *Crimes of the Century* for TV. I truly loved performing in these shows, the adrenaline would be running wild as I would be axed to death or poisoned. Sometimes I managed to stay alive.

But my performance days weren't over. Little did I know, I would end up performing more than 2,000 times as a marriage commissioner, a conduit of joy and love. That was the best choice that I made for my retirement career.

Who knew that it would almost become a full-time job for quite a number of years? To this day, I get such a high on each wedding day and thoroughly enjoy the whole process from when I get up in the morning, to getting ready for the wedding, to going to the venue and performing the service. The thing that made me the happiest was that Bob was able to travel on this exciting journey with me, as he too would look forward to our exciting weekends

The playful child in Edna.

CHAPTER 4:
DEARLY BELOVED

I was so excited when I received a phone call for the first wedding. I arranged to have an interview with them prior to the ceremony. Right from the moment when they arrived, I thought they were a young, smiling, optimistic, carefree couple head over heels in love with each other, and he was so good looking. I was happy to find that they were eloping with just the groom's sister, the bride's twin sister, and their significant others in attendance. That was a real plus for me to see how this was going to play out. I always ask how a couple met to get to know their background and get them to tell me their story. It is so interesting to hear, and of course, I would always ask more questions. I loved that this couple opened up to me and kept talking. They told me that they met May 2, 1992, at her high school graduation party out in a small-town farmyard. Pam had heard of John from her twin sister who worked with him. On their first meeting, John came up hugging and congratulating Pam thinking she was her twin sister. Pam had no clue who he was. Jon was convinced that Pam was her twin sister. He had seen photos of Pam and thought she looked a lot different than her sister. She had to drag him off slightly annoyed and leave him standing stunned with her twin sister. It was not love at first sight.

They bumped into each other one more time that year

and had a great evening chatting, laughing, and parting with a goodbye kiss. Then Pam moved to Alberta and BC. No cell phones, no conversations. Over the time Pam was away, her twin would mention him, or Pam would casually ask about him every once in a while, how's John? Fast forward to summer 1994, she came back to Saskatchewan. I asked, "When you came back how did you get together again?"

She shared with me that shortly after she moved home, she and Jon randomly bumped into each other with her twin sister by her side, no less. From then on, they were together. No dates were arranged or spoken, they just met up again in her hometown and just became best friends, laughing and falling in love. John never asked Pam to be his girlfriend it was just that they were together. It was natural that they were a couple now. "Were you serious about each other?" I asked. By the next summer they had already planned to be married, I guess that answered my question.

They did everything together and were just happy being, loving, living, and going with the flow. They wanted to be married but did not want a big ordeal. They didn't even tell people they were engaged for months. "How did John propose to you?" I asked, curiously. In December 1995, after Pam finished work and John was waiting to drive her home, he said, "Let's get married next weekend just go the two of us." Ecstatic and giddy with love, Pam said, "Yes, but I can't, I'm writing exams this week." He said, "Next weekend." Deal, the two young kids in love, crazy happy to start a life as husband and wife. They decided to have her twin sister and partner as their witnesses, and Pam convinced John they should have someone from his family to keep the peace when they surprised everyone.

They happened to pick me from a list of marriage commissioners. Here they were oh so young and nervous of the steps to be taken so quickly and I so apprehensive and excited at the same time. From when they entered my home, I found myself emotionally involved with this special young couple. They asked if I knew of a place, although I had never been to The City of Regina Greenhouse, I heard it was a beautiful place with flowers and trees for small weddings and suggested they check it out. As both John and Pam loved plants, this was the perfect place. At the end of our meeting at my kitchen table, I said, "I wasn't going to mention this but since you are such a nice young couple, I will tell you that this is going to be my first time that I will be performing a marriage ceremony." John placed his hand on my arm and without missing a beat smiling replied, "That's ok, it's our first time too."

A week later I arrived all excited still in my Mrs. Claus outfit from a prior commitment. This was much to their delight, but I changed into my brand-new robe that I had custom made. I remembered being nervous but proud of how things went. The couple were so attentive listening to every word I spoke. I was on such a high I knew then that this was my calling. For the first time I saw this beautiful venue with all the trees and flowers I never knew existed. I immediately decided that I would become a volunteer here upon my retirement from SGI.

Over the years I kept in touch with John and Pam and found that they were a perfect team going through their days happy and easy going. Content, seldom apart, and full of smiles. They loved their life together, they never fought, sometimes annoyed but truly close connected friends full of hopes and dreams one day at a time. Four years after performing their marriage ceremony, I had the opportunity to perform Pam's twin sister's wedding. After the ceremony Pam approached me and said, "You may be more confident and polished now but you were so special at our wedding because we were your first couple."

A year later, Pam wrote me a letter advising me that they had purchased a home and had moved to the town of Earl Grey and didn't want me to lose touch with them. Sadly, John was diagnosed with malignant melanoma the next December 1997. I couldn't fathom that such a beautiful couple was struck with such tragic news within such a short time together. I felt so sad. He faced each day with strength and smiles. The ups and downs of cancer are a challenge, but they stayed strong and hopeful together and carried on. I would hear from Pam again and she would tell me that John was in remission.

I met their little angel, Eric John, the day I married Pam's twin sister; he was such a sweetheart. He was John's fight, light, hope, and strength. Most never knew how sick John was because he never wanted attention and bounced back after each round. John gave such meaning to the word "courage," quiet and strong he fought. I could never imagine how their life changed for them and admired them for the courage and strength they had. The three of them shared a bond that was deep.

Eric was at all of John's chemo treatments and his surgeries. Eric was a quiet, gentle soul and was content around it all. He kept John fighting. However, love never dies. They had an amazingly too short of a journey but bursting with adventure and love beyond measure. John is her hero and still gives her strength. Forever missed and always loved.

I was devastated when I heard that John had lost his battle to cancer on February 16, 2001. Bob and I were both adamant about attending John's celebration of life. Much to our great disappointment a terrible Saskatchewan storm hit Regina the morning of his celebration and we debated on whether we should venture out. Sadly, we decided for our safety, not to attend. Pam and John are forever in my heart, and I am so grateful that they were my first couple that started my journey in my new career as a marriage commissioner.

My Second Wedding

My second wedding was like jumping from the frying pan into the fire. Shortly after my first wedding, Bob and I were at a restaurant having dinner with friends when I saw Bill Heidt, Vice President OF SGI, and his fiancée sitting a couple of booths over. I was so excited I couldn't wait to tell them of my new career as a marriage commissioner and to show them the pictures that I had brought with me to show our friends of my first wedding. To my total surprise they swore me to secrecy and asked me to perform their marriage ceremony for them which they planned to have in a fairly short time. They had started looking for someone but were not quite sure of who they wanted and were happy to have someone they knew. I was on cloud nine. They also advised me that the best man would be Don Black, the past president of SGI, another reason to be nervous.

On the day of the wedding, I was nervous. While getting ready to leave to do the ceremony my nose bled and I couldn't stop it. We did everything that we could think of, but it continued to bleed. I thought I might have to call ahead and let them know I would be late, finally we managed to get it stopped and away we went.

While we were driving to their place, I became so calm. The nervousness left with the blood. As I was performing their ceremony, I noticed the groom was so nervous that as he was reading his vows the paper crackled, he was shaking so badly. I was tempted to tell him to go have a nosebleed. Being my second wedding and marrying an important couple, I worked hard at not being intimidated. I was focused on my ceremony as I didn't want to be perceived as an inexperienced marriage commissioner. It was important for me to be professional. I believe because I was so calm that I was successful in doing that. This experience gave me confidence to go forward. I was starting to get the hang of my new career and I was thoroughly enjoying it.

By becoming a marriage commissioner, I was quickly introduced to unexpected scenarios and ideas and often delightful endings. Here is an example of such an ending. After performing a ceremony at the Hotel Saskatchewan, the bride and groom made a dramatic exit. A flock of white doves were released as the couple stood on the steps to begin their life together. As I witnessed the release of the doves, it was like love floating in the air with the couple walking beneath. What a beautiful sight.

The oldest couple I ever married was an eighty-three-year-old bride and a seventy-nine- year-old groom. At the interview I said to them, "You have had so many life experiences, what can I possibly say to you that you have not already heard." The bride to be looked at me and said,

"Just say something nice." I said to her, "Ok, I can do that." That was an easy order for me to fill.

Another elderly couple from out of town decided to elope without telling any of their family members. They asked me if I could supply witnesses for them.

They almost got caught the morning they were packing their belongings in the living room when her daughter showed up at their house unannounced. She grabbed the suitcase ran to the bedroom to make sure the daughter would not see it and she tucked it under the bed.

I was giggling when they were telling us their story as I could see myself doing the same thing and feeling guilty. Just as they were ready to leave while putting their luggage in the trunk of their vehicle, his son shows up. It was difficult to keep a straight face and act normal when they felt so guilty for doing this behind their children's backs. All the way to Regina they kept looking back to see if anyone was following them. They finally arrived at their hotel in the city. For the first time that day they were able to relax.

They changed their clothes into their wedding attire and came to the house looking lovely and giddy with excitement that they had pulled this off without anyone finding out.

My son Shawn and daughter-in-law Rosanne were the witnesses. As they faced one another I could see the happiness on their faces and their smiles as they said their vows to each other. While they were telling their story, Bob poured a glass of wine for each of us, and we drank to their happiness as they spoke with excitement that they were now husband and wife. Now, to tell the children.

One wonders how lasagna would have the power to change a reception venue. Mine certainly wouldn't, but this mother of the groom did. It was a beautiful wedding involving two high-profile businesspeople from the community and was held at the Hotel Saskatchewan here in Regina. The groom's three children walked him up the aisle while the bride's two sons walked her up the aisle. After the ceremony the venue changed to Little Flower Church for the reception. The hotel would not allow them to bring in their food. The grooms Italian mother wanted to serve her lasagna that she made for all the guests at the supper.

My husband and I were invited since I was involved with both the bride and groom through the business world. I can still taste the lasagna that felt like silk when you swallowed it. As we were in line to sign in at the reception, two women behind us were talking about the ceremony and how the marriage commissioner spoke to the parents and then to the guests. It made them feel so inclusive. They did not know it was me in front of them since I was no longer in my robe. It was nice to hear what people were saying behind my back.

High Society Wedding

Performing one of my high-profile weddings in Regina, I suspected that there would be some big names in attendance, but I never for the life of me, imagined how big it was going to be. The likes of Victor Sawa, the maestro for the Regina Symphony Orchestra, performed throughout the reception. Ed Lewis, music director for the University of Regina, played during the ceremony. Joe Fafard, our local world-famous artist, was in attendance. I always wished I had one of his infamous cow sculptures. Wilf Perreault, another local artist, famous for his back-alley paintings which I do have hanging on my wall. However, the guest that stood out the most for me was Jacqui Schumiatcher. She was dressed meticulously as always. A recipient of the Order of Canada and the Saskatchewan Order of Merit, her sustained philanthropy contributed immeasurably to the vitality of the province's arts and culture scene. When she first approached me at the reception I was quite nervous to speak to her. As the conversation continued, I became less intimidated as she made me feel comfortable. All of her great accomplishments made her a interesting person to talk to.

I met the bride, Michelle Hunter through work. She was the banquet coordinator for Hotel Saskatchewan. We saw each other quite often through business and became friends. I was always excited to be invited to join her for lunch at the hotel. We would often exchange stories about our experiences in our line of work. I always teased my staff that I had a luncheon engagement at Hotel Saskatchewan.

She was always able to get a hold of me for our lunch dates, except for the one time she needed to contact me to perform the marriage for her and her fiancé, Brad Hunter. I was missing in action. She could not get a hold of me. After a couple of weeks, by calling and calling, Brad mentioned to her that maybe they should get his friend a judge to marry them. Michelle said, "Give me one more week. I want Edna to perform our ceremony." Finally, much to her delight, I answered my phone. Bob and I had been away on vacation in Arizona. I was thrilled to be asked and excited to be performing their marriage ceremony.

The wedding ceremony was held at Hotel Saskatchewan Radisson Plaza in the Saskatchewan room. I ended the ceremony with, "I now have the pleasure of introducing to you for the first time as husband and wife, Mr. and Mrs. Brad and Michelle Hunter and Hunter. Both of their last names were Hunter. It got a good laugh from the crowd.

As everyone was going through the receiving line after the ceremony, a judge asked Michelle, "Where did Edna get her service from?" Michelle told him that I authored it myself. He couldn't believe it. I knew that I shone at that service for a judge to want to know where I got my ceremony.

The reception was an elegant affair held in the ballroom that was decorated beautifully. It was a stand-up reception with the various food stations situated around the room. There was a carving station with roast beef and roast lamb. A seafood station with various kinds of seafood, a canapé station, and a dessert station with a chocolate fountain and an assortment of dainties.

To this day, I am glad that I wasn't privy to the names of the guests on the invitation list. I am certain that the ceremony would not have gone as smoothly as it did. My voice would have given my nervousness away I am sure.

Edna at Hotel Saskatchewan.

It was a busy time with only six marriage commissioners in Regina. People were phoning back two to three times a day and begging to please do their wedding at the most unusual time of day since that was the only time that would be left. All the marriage commissioners had the same problem.

One morning I got a phone call from a fellow who

wanted me to do a wedding for his fiancée and him at 1:00 p.m., it was one hour out of town. I told him I could not do it for him at 1:00 p.m. since I was booked for the better part of the day. He said, "Ok, I will get someone else." I said, "That's great," and jokingly said, "but I am the best there is." We laughed and said goodbye.

About two weeks later, the same fellow called again and said, "I am calling the best there is." In reality, the rest of the marriage commissioners were booked solid and would not take any more weddings for that day. He sounded so desperate at this time that I reluctantly agreed to do it at 10:30 a.m. one hour out of Regina. We were up early that Saturday to get my hair done and have breakfast. We were on the road by 9:30 a.m., Bob and I wondered how we were going to make it through the day, since I needed traveling time to get back to Kiwanis Waterfall Gardens for my second wedding, followed by the third wedding at Hotel Saskatchewan, and the fourth at the Band Stand. The fifth at a private backyard, then back to Kiwanis for my sixth wedding, and finally the seventh, my last wedding for the day was approximately one hour out of town again. We managed to be on time most of the day, but I had to call ahead on our way to the last wedding to advise them I would be about twenty minutes late.

That was the biggest day in my career as a marriage commissioner. My husband Bob, who was my wingman, stood by me through it all but was ready to hire a plane. Yet, by the end of the day, I felt exhilarated and on such a high with such a great sense of accomplishment. By the end of that summer, it was starting to take a toll on us since I was doing anywhere from three to five weddings every weekend. It became a full-time job. By the next summer however, there were ten more marriage commissioners appointed and we no longer had that problem, much to our relief.

CHAPTER 5:
I PROMISE TO ACCEPT YOU, PROTECT YOU, AND LOVE YOU

I performed a number of weddings within one family. Within the structure of about five different families, I became the go-to marriage commissioner, marrying aunts, then a nephew, the mother, a cousin, and everything in-between. If I hit a homerun at the first wedding, I was often referred to other family members. Because of this, Bob and I developed close bonds as these special people became like family to us. Within one particular family relationship, I performed five marriage ceremonies over a period of years within one family dynamic. We became like part of the family and were invited to all of their receptions.

Finally, the fifth wedding was the last one in that generation to be married. I was told I will have to wait for the next generation to come along before I can do another wedding for this family. I will never forget the ring bearer at the first wedding that I did for this family. It was within the first year of becoming a marriage commissioner. He was such a cutie with the biggest puppy dog eyes I had ever seen. There was much excitement as the ceremony was about to begin however, there was some concern as to how their four-year-old, their wild child Tanner was going to behave. He was the ring bearer. Gramma Debbie was especially concerned. I knelt down to meet his eyes and said, "You have an important job to do and that is to hold the rings until I ask for them and you will then give them to me. You are going to make Mommy and Daddy and Gramma Debbie really proud for doing this important job." Everything was going along great, and he was wondering when he was going to be asked to give the ring to me. I looked over at him several times, he never took his big brown eyes off me. He continued to stare right at me as if to say, "Ask me already." Finally, I asked, "Tanner, have you the wedding rings?" He literally ran over and handed me the rings with the biggest smile on his face. I gave him a high-five. A job well done.

Years later I received a phone call from the family, letting me know that their mother had passed away. They asked if I would perform her grave-side service. I said, "I marry people, I don't bury them." They said, "This is important to us, can we please come and see you?" and I agreed. They told me that their mother was at every wedding that I did for their families and she enjoyed every one of them. She became fond of me. They did not have a church affiliation and couldn't think of anyone better to do her graveside service. I had grown fond of these family members so I put some extra thought into their request and decided that if I can do a wedding surely to God, I could do a celebration of life.

The family arrived at the gravesite and I began with these words.

"We are gathered here today to do honour to the life and memory of Vivian Vera Soutar, who was born on December 20, 1929, and left this earth on June 15, 2012.

It is a life that we are here to celebrate. Today we will place in our memories the treasures of this life. Her virtues, her victories, and her vision. These will remain untarnished in our minds and so live on.

We rejoice that she lives on in a special way in her children, grandchildren, and great grandchildren."

I did a biblical reading, Doug her son gave the eulogy, Lindsay her granddaughter read a meaningful poem. There was some time given for anyone who wanted to reflect and remember some fond or funny or serious memories of Mom and Grandma. Don her son did the committal. The words spoken were "Here under this wide and open sky she will rest in peace. And we dedicate this simple plot amid these natural surroundings to every beautiful and precious memory." Roses were placed by the Urn.

After the Lord's Prayer, my closing words were, "Now let us go in the quietness of spirit to face whatever may be ahead with cheerfulness, with courage and with fortitude.

We rejoice that she lives on in a special way in her children, grandchildren and great grandchildren."

Although it is my more forte to marry people and not bury them, it was an honour for me to do this service. During my wedding ceremonies I am called upon to unite a couple in the beginning of their life together. It is always filled with happiness. Reflecting on a celebration of life I am reminded that there is also ceremony in the ending of one's life. It can be filled with a sense of sadness and loss, but it is also filled with deep reverence for that person's life and what they meant to those they loved and left behind. Looking back, I feel grateful to have been involved in both the beginning of a life's journey and the ending of a life's journey, thus completing the circle of life.

Marriage involves more than just the couple uniting, it involves families who may or may not support their decision. Family members can also play an integral role in how the ceremony unfolds. One day I received a phone call on my noon hour while I was at work. A couple had just picked up their marriage license and asked if I could perform their ceremony the next day which was Friday afternoon. Since they were already downtown, I told them to come and meet with me right away. They had been together for quite some time. As the groom shared information about marrying the love of his life, his children, who lived out of province, were not in agreement for their wealthy father to marry anyone, let alone her. Things got bad when he told them they were going to marry soon regardless. The children decided to come to Regina on the weekend to talk their father out of marrying this woman. The couple came to my house the next day which was Friday at 4:00 p.m. and I performed the ceremony for them.

After midnight while they were sleeping upstairs in their house, there was a commotion in the lower level, his children had arrived. It was not a pretty sight. The children ended up abruptly leaving, vowing never to return again. The couple had a large church wedding two months later to which my husband and I were invited. They were a happy couple. Shortly after their church ceremony, the bride and I were in the same hair salon. We were happy to see one another again. I wanted to know how they were doing. She never mentioned anything about his children, but she did say to me, "I am so happy. He may not be the best-looking guy, but he is mine."

One of my most heartfelt moments was when the bride chose her two-year-old son to walk her down the aisle. He walked proudly beside his mom. I thought it was the cutest thing that I had ever seen. When I asked the question, "Who gives this woman to be married to this man?" He responded with, "Me." I could hardly contain my emotions. I was blinking madly to keep the tears from falling. The bride smiled looking down at him and gave him a fist pump as if to say, "Good job," and then gave him a huge hug. The groom met them partway down the aisle and gave him a big hug and passed him on to his grandma. As he turned to the bride, she took his arm, and they walked the rest of the way together. I whispered to them, "Ever so cute," I then asked them to join hands and the ceremony began.

In August of 2007, I was curious when my granddaughter Laura and her Fiancée Quenton called to see me, wondering what the purpose of their visit might be. I was surprised and elated when they asked me if I would perform their marriage ceremony. Since the talk was that they were going to be married in the Anglican Church. I was honoured to have the pleasure of performing their marriage ceremony that was being held in beautiful Kiwanis Waterfall Gardens. The day was cloudy and kind of drizzling all morning. By early afternoon it was starting to clear. As my son walked his daughter down the steps at Kiwanis the sun came out for the first time that day. What a beautiful sight. This was quite a large wedding. When I started my opening remarks and went on to say how special this wedding was to me, I became emotional. My granddaughter, the bride, said, "Gramma don't cry" I pulled myself together and carried on giving them a nice ceremony for them to remember. The reception was in a beautifully decorated hall and a fun evening was had by all. They have two lovely children, a girl Kara and a boy Alex.

Father of the bride (Rod) walking his daughter (Laura) down the steps at Kiwanis Park.

Laura and Quenton with marriage commissioner grandma.

In late afternoon on July 31, 2020, I received a phone call from my second granddaughter from the same family Kirsten. She asked me if I would marry her and Nathan on August 1, 2020, since it was their fifteenth anniversary of their first date. I was shocked, I said, "That's tomorrow." She responded with, "Yes, it is," I immediately advised her that the first thing that must happen if they wanted to get married the next day was to get their marriage license that day. Would you believe it? They called me with the marriage license number within the hour.

Because of the short notice only the parents of the bride and groom were in attendance. It was a beautiful evening, and the wedding was being held at the end of a long boardwalk overlooking the legislative building. It was such a precious time for me to be able to do it for them since they had been together for fifteen years and engaged for five. We enjoyed a lovely dinner at The Fireside Restaurant afterward. How is this for an odd coincidence? Kirsten and Nathan had recently purchased a home. The house number was the same as Nathan's age and the street name was Nathan Street. The family all thought that this was so cool. Their home is so suited to them, and they are a happy little family. Knight, their cat, runs the show.

Kirsten and Nathan on their wedding day at Wascana Park.

Bride and groom with her parents Rod and Liz.

Blending of Families

Sand Ceremony

The wedding took place at the Ramada Hotel. There were about 200 invited guests. The bride had four children and the groom had three. The children's ages were between four to fourteen years. The children rehearsed their part in the wedding the night before and were excited and eager to play their role in the wedding. I, too, was anxious to see how they would do. I performed the ceremony as per the couples wishes. After, I pronounced the bride and groom to be husband and wife and said, "You may now seal your vows with a kiss," the kids giggled, and the younger children jumped up since they knew their part came right after the kiss. The older children grabbed them to sit down and waited to be called.

There were nine vases of sand sitting on the table. One black for the groom, one white for the bride, and seven of each color: red, yellow, purple, green, pink, blue, and brown. I felt excited for them since I never saw so much excitement as they eagerly waited at the edge of their seats as I began the sand ceremony.

We now celebrate the bride and groom's union with a symbolic sand ceremony. First, they will pour their sand as they commit their lives to each other, representing the strong foundation of their relationship. That foundation includes their children that come with them into this marriage, and all the important steps on their journeys. This foundation will support them in their love as they grow and change together.

One, representing you, Groom, and all that you were and all that you are, and all that you will ever be. Pours half of the black sand from his vase into the centre vase.

One representing you, Bride, and all that you were and all that you are, and all that you will ever be. Pours half of the white sand into the centre vase.

I then include the children from the oldest to the youngest.

"The Bride and Groom would like to recognize their children and their importance in this marriage which is symbolized through the pouring of these individual vases of sand."

One representing your first child's name and all that you were and all that you are, and all that you will ever be. Pours half of the sand in the vase. When it came to the youngest's turn, the fourteen-year-old immediately picked her up so she could take her vase and pour half her sand in the centre vase. When he set her down she said out loud "I did it, I did it."

This was repeated until all the children had poured all their sand in the centre vase.

Then the bride and groom topped it off with each of them pouring the remainder of the sand into the centre vase. I continued with,

"You have now blended the sand together symbolizing the uniting of your two lives and the lives of your children, and that you will be there to nurture and support them.

Just as these grains of sand can never be separated and poured again into individual vases, so will your marriage be blended into one family."

Another Favourite Ceremony of Mine Is the Rose Ceremony

Twenty-two years ago, a physician was referred to a cardiologist. At that appointment, the physician met a cardiology technologist who prepared him for a cardiac stress test with the cardiologist.

One year later, a follow-up appointment was made with the same cardiologist and the *physician* met *her* again. He did not miss this second chance to ask her on a casual date. She said, yes.

Three years later, he proposed to her in the Hotel Saskatchewan lounge.

After another three years, they called to ask if I would perform their marriage ceremony.

The groom picked the venue and date in reference to his English heritage where he was previously employed as the Physician for the Queen's children while on the Royal Tour in the NWT.

They were married on Victoria Day, May 21, 2006 in the Royal Suite of the Hotel Saskatchewan in Regina (also known as the Queen's suite).

Pat and Keith have three children each, ages ten to nineteen years. Two boys and a girl. None of the children had ever attended a wedding, so to make the event special for them, they were the wedding party. This was a private family wedding. Gowns were custom made for the girls and the boys wore tuxes.

Pat's eldest son Jesse was her man-of-honor. Brandon and Tonya were in the wedding party on their mom's side. Keith's eldest son Miles was his best man. Clare and Ted were in the wedding party on their dad's side.

As I began the ceremony, I asked, "Who presents the bride and groom to be married to each other?"

The children replied in unison "We do."

At the appropriate time in the ceremony, I did the recognition of the children and the blending of the two families with these words.

In the elegant language of flowers red roses are a symbol of love, and the giving of a single red rose is a clear and unmistakable way of saying the words, "I love you." For this reason, it is fitting that the first gift you exchange as husband and wife be the gift of a single red rose. The bride and groom exchange roses and say, "I love you" to each other, they place the roses in a vase, and both hold the vase as I continue.

Often marriage is viewed as the union of two people. In reality marriage is much broader. It is always a joining of families. As part of the family nature of this marriage, the bride and groom would like to recognize each of the children Jesse, Miles, Brandon, Clare, Tonya and Ted, and their significance in this marriage. By placing a rose in a single vase by each of the children represents that your lives are joined together which signifies the blending of your two families to one.

The evening was enjoyed with forty invited guests in the Royal Suite to celebrate their special day. The bride arranged a surprise visit by a Queen impersonator who entertained the guests with a humorous speech to end the evening.

Pat and Keith.

Bride, groom, and their children performing the rose ceremony.

Vows to Children

I would often get emotional watching the parents pledge their love and loyalty to one another's children, but nothing struck me quite like the following pledge from the groom to his bride's son. The wedding was in the wide-open spaces behind the Lady Slipper Courtyard at 1:30 p.m. on a very, hot July day. The Grandparents had to be relocated to the shaded area even before the ceremony had started. I performed my usual ceremony and as always included the children. I gave the parents choices for the optional ceremony and the parents selected they wanted to make a commitment to the children by saying vows to them.

At the appropriate time I proceeded with this part of the ceremony which is a recognition to the children.

"As part of the family nature of this marriage, James and Mallory would like to recognize Taylor and Eleanor and their significance in this marriage with special vows and presentation."

Mallory (has a seven-year-old son Taylor from a previous relationship and they have a one-year-old daughter Eleanor together)

The bride said her vows to both children. "Taylor, and Eleanor we promise to be supportive and loving parents, we will love you and respect you for who you are, each of you will always be an important part of our family. Today as we face a new future together, as a symbol of our love and commitment that we have for us as a family, we would like to give each of you a special gift." Presents Eleanor her gift.

Groom: (Speaks only to Taylor as he gets down to meet him at his eye level) "Taylor, I promise to accept you, and to protect and love you all my life. I promise to do my best to guide and support you. To respect you enough to allow you to see the world through your eyes." Presents Taylor his gift. To which the guests rose and applauded.

It's moments like these that I get so emotional often struggling to keep the tears from flowing down my cheeks.

James, Mallory, Taylor, and Eleanor.

CHAPTER 6:
MAY MY ARMS BE YOUR SHELTER AND MY HEART BE YOUR HOME

When a wedding invitation arrives, there is an immediate anticipation for the big day. What are we going to wear? Booking the day off work or clearing our calendar. What will the bride wear? Who will I see at the wedding? I wonder if so and so is invited? I sure hope so, then we will have someone to sit with at the reception. It will be great to see some of my long-lost relatives. These are all thoughts we think as well as the thought of having to sit with relatives we are not all that excited to see. I am sure these were some of the thoughts that the guests at this particular wedding were thinking. All the guests had arrived, the groom and his attendants were patiently waiting inside the venue. The bride, along with her attendants, were excitedly waiting in the party bus. It was getting close to the time the ceremony was to start and the bride's mom had not yet arrived. The bride wondered where her mom was. As it got close to the time for the ceremony to begin, family members panicked and called different people to try to locate her. No luck.

Eventually the sister of the bride went outside of the bus and happened to look down the row of vehicles and suddenly recognized her mother's car. She immediately ran down the row of vehicles. When she reached her mother's car she found her slumped over the steering wheel unconscious. She ran into the hall and screamed, "Is there a doctor in here?" Several people from the medical profession came to their assistance and did what they could. An ambulance was called, and the family had to decide what to do. The father and the sister, who was a designated bridesmaid, went with the ambulance to the hospital. He asked his brother, the bride's uncle, to walk his daughter down the aisle in place of him.

The groom was a nervous wreck. He started walking back and forth, clasping his hands, and demonstrating great anxiety. The bride and groom decided to go ahead with the wedding but asked me to make my ceremony brief. As I walked up the aisle to the front of the venue, I was breathing deeply to keep control of my emotions. As I recall, I addressed the guests letting them know that there is a family emergency and that we will be starting the ceremony before too long. It was hard for me to think clearly as I got busy striking out a lot of my material. I couldn't believe this was happening and I wondered if I was going to be able to perform the ceremony without breaking down myself.

It was time to begin the ceremony. I had gained my composure as I knew this young couple were going to need all the love and support, they could get. As the groom walked down the aisle I was concerned that he would completely fall apart. However, he did manage to make it to the front without breaking down. The bridesmaids walked sadly down the aisle on a normally happy occasion. As the bride entered on her uncles' arm, I can only imagine what she was thinking or how she was feeling. I am sure she was wishing that it could have been her father walking her down the aisle, that her sister could have been her support as her bridesmaid and that her mother could have looked lovingly and proudly at her beautiful daughter on her most special day. But that is not how this couples wedding day unfolded. The bride bravely made her way up to the front with a half-frozen smile on her face that never changed. They stopped at the front row as planned and I asked, "Who gives this woman to be married to this man?" The uncle was unsure as what to say. With some coaching he uttered the words "I do." The groom joined his bride and together they proceeded to take their places at the front. My feeling was that they managed to get here without falling apart which gave me the courage to give them a brief but loving service. The bride's expression never changed, and I am sure she was in total shock. The groom had great difficulty controlling his emotions. However, we all managed to get through it. I am not sure if anyone in attendance was able to take in my words. The main concern was the well-being of the bride's mother. The reception was a sad occasion and ended right after the meal.

Immediately after performing this extremely emotional and heart wrenching marriage ceremony, my husband and I got into the car, and we drove to the next wedding that I had scheduled only one hour after this wedding. Despite what I had just experienced I needed to turn my thoughts and attention to the next wedding and be ready to perform the ceremony for this next couple as if nothing dramatic had just happened. However, when we arrived in the parking lot and got out of the vehicle, this bride's mother, who knew the mother of the bride from the last wedding, came running over to tell us that she had died. As Bob is a man of few words, he put his arm around me, giving me the strength and support that I would need to get me through this wedding. I left behind everything that had just happened. I walked up the aisle as if it was the first ceremony for me that day. My strength was that I did not want to disappoint this couple by displaying my emotions and overshadowing the joy and excitement of their wedding day. I don't know how, but I managed to pull it off. Bob and I drove home in silence, deep in our thoughts. When we arrived home, Bob poured me a glass of wine. Within minutes, I was ready for the second glass. I put this day to rest by sending my prayers, thoughts and love to the family that went through this trying experience.

CHAPTER 7:
HONOURING CULTURES

Through my experiences as a marriage commissioner, I was lucky to learn about a variety of cultural traditions. I not only participated in their traditions but witnessed how they honoured and continued these traditions on the most important day of their life. I had a couple ask me to perform their ceremony. The bride spoke English and the groom spoke both English and German. He advised me that his parents would be coming from Germany to attend the wedding. With a German background and being able to speak the language, I suggested to the groom that he say his vows in German so his parents would be able to understand his vows as he spoke them to his bride. I had a friend who is fluent in the German language assist me in preparing the vows.

The bride said her vows in English and the groom said his vows in German, repeating after me. His parents were in tears with happiness to be able to understand that their son was saying the same vows in German as his bride was in English.

They rushed up to me after the ceremony and thanked, and hugged, and kissed me for doing this for them. Beside their son, I was the probably the only one who could carry on a conversation with them as I understand German but struggled with communicating with them since I am no longer fluent in German.

I was involved with another multicultural wedding consisting of a German bride and an East Indian groom who was attending university in Germany. Since the German Government has poor relations with India they would not approve them to get married and through negotiations it would have cost them a fortune. The bride has an aunt living in Regina. Her aunt contacted me and made arrangements for me to marry them in my home. I had just sold my house and all the furnishings as I was preparing to relocate into a retirement community. After arriving from Germany, I performed their ceremony in an empty house. The house may have been empty, but it was still a special occasion. The aunt brought over a beautifully decorated cake and other dainties. Because of this couple's desire to be together as husband and wife they found a way to make that happen. After the ceremony, they went on a holiday to B.C. before returning home to Germany.

Another custom that I was involved with was the breaking of the glass in the Jewish tradition. I performed my regular ceremony with their choice of marriage vows. After pronouncing them husband and wife and sealing their vows with a kiss, the following Jewish custom, the breaking of the glass, was performed. Prior to the breaking of the glass, I read the following words that I obtained from the internet that spoke to the meaningfulness of this custom.

"The breaking of the glass at the end of a wedding ceremony serves to remind us of two important aspects of a marriage. The bride and groom – and everyone – should consider these marriage vows as an irrevocable act – just as permanent and final as the breaking of this glass is unchangeable. But the breaking of the glass also is a warning of the frailty of a marriage. That sometimes a single thoughtless act, breach of trust, or infidelity can damage a marriage in ways that are difficult to undo – just as it would be so difficult to undo the breaking of this glass.

Knowing that this marriage is permanent, the bride and groom should strive to show each other the love and respect befitting their spouse and love of their life." Then the Groom broke the glass which was in a cloth bag. He does so by stomping on it.

The guests then yelled "Mazel tov" which means "good luck" in Hebrew, once the glass is broken. When they had originally said they were going to perform this custom, I asked "Are you not afraid that there is going to be glass all over the place." They laughed and said, "No need to worry, the glass will be placed in a cloth bag." Again, I learned something new.

High Filipino Tradition

I have performed several Filipino weddings however there was only one with the high Filipino tradition. These customs have enriched my experience as a marriage commissioner. What intrigued me about this tradition was the number of people who actively participated. In most ceremonies, you only have one witness for each the bride and the groom but in the Filipino tradition, there is a meaningful role for numerous people to fulfill. It adds additional support to the commitment that the couple are making. There are eight sets of primary sponsors who signed an elaborate marriage book. The three sets of secondary sponsors each had their responsibilities. One set were candle sponsors who were responsible for lighting the taper candle in preparation for the bride and groom to light their unity candle. The second set were the veil sponsors who would place the veil over the bride's head and the groom's shoulder. Picture a big burly football player type guy with this elegant veil draped over his shoulders. The third set were cord sponsors who placed the cord over their heads onto their shoulders. And then there was a young lad who was the coin bearer. He passed the coins to me which I in turn placed into the palm of the bride and grooms' hands. They then cupped their hands together which symbolized their unity. I don't recall going into this much detail at the rehearsal, yet each one knew precisely what they needed to do, and they did it to perfection.

Iskcon Regina: Hindu Marriage Traditions

I received a phone call from Dr. Jai L. Ram inquiring about making an appointment to meet with a young Hindu couple. Right from the beginning, we were comfortable with one another. After that, he referred me to many other couples that I performed the wedding ceremony for. The following story, as told by Dr. Jai L. Ram gives you a peek of what it is like to be married in the Hindu culture and what it was like for me to be a part of that.

To give you some background information, India is a vast country, a sub-continent, with many religious traditions and practices. Over a 1,000 years ago, the main religion was *Santana Dharma,* now known as Hinduism. Over the years, the population composition has changed, and so have the religious practices. As a result, the religious ceremonies and rites have also undergone many changes. However, today about 80% of Indians, practice Hinduism. Therefore, the following applies only to Hindu marriage practices and rituals.

A Hindu marriage signifies a couple's commitment to one another in the presence of God and the joining together of two families. The actual marriage traditions are elaborate and can take anywhere from one day to two weeks. The first Hindu wedding in a temple was a unique experience for me to participate in this type of ceremony. Upon entering the Iskcon Temple, here in Regina, we were asked to take our shoes off. I was happy to comply but I have to admit I had never performed a ceremony in bare feet before, so it was a new experience for me. I was sure glad that I had a pedicure the day before and my toenails were nicely polished, thank goodness. I was immediately in awe of the Hindu cultural display at the front of the temple with its Gods and Goddess and beautiful and colourful adornment. I was advised at that time that I must never have my back toward this display. With that, the couple and I, and their witnesses, stood sideways facing one another. The service was coordinated with both me and Dr. Jai L. Ram who delivered the Hindu cultural ceremony and words of wisdom, and I delivered not only the legal aspect of the ceremony, but a heartfelt and meaningful charge to the couple. It was an honor as a Caucasian woman to be invited into the Hindu temple to participate in their cultural wedding.

As they continue with the more traditional aspect of the ceremony, on the final and most important day of celebrations a Mandap, or marriage canopy, is erected. The couple, the priest, and close family members are seated within this beautiful sacred space, during which the wedding vows are taken. There are fourteen components to a Hindu wedding ceremony which are performed before a Havan or sacred ritual fire. The most important part of the ceremony is entitled Sapta-Padi or "walking seven steps together." The couple take seven steps circumambulating the Havan. Each step symbolizes a different marriage vow reflecting the qualities of the couple's commitment to one another. A step toward the necessities of life, a step toward strength and vigor, a step toward prosperity, a step toward welfare and total well-being, a step toward progeny, a step toward good seasons throughout their lives, and a final step toward a lifelong friendship. These commitments are made in the presence of God and with the blessings of family members and loved ones.

Once the actual ceremony has been completed, the newly married couple sign the marriage registry which is witnessed by two other people. The celebration continues with a reception that includes an elaborate meal, speeches, and of course, dancing and music.

After the ceremony at the Iskcon Temple was over, it was insisted that Bob and I stay for the feast. The women brought an enormous amount and variety of delicious Indian food, so delicious. What amazed me was how they all sat on the floor in a straight line to eat the food. Bob was unable to sit on the floor, so we were given the most luxurious seat in the temple which was a soft and comfortable love seat. I was asked to perform other Hindu ceremonies on a number of occasions to which I was honoured each and every time.

It was important to me to share my experiences with various cultures to give everyone some insight into how other cultures and religious traditions conduct their most important life rituals. The love shared by a couple is sacred and is affirmed during these ancient spiritual practices.

Hindu Temple.

Edna and Jia performing the ceremony together.

Muslim Culture: Life Is Truly Laziz – Their Happily Ever After
Laila Hirani and Aziz Sabuwala

I am proud to share this Muslim story with you as told by Laila Hirani and me as we embarked on their marriage journey. Aziz and Laila met online. He was in India, and she was in Canada. Ironically, it was their mutual hatred for getting married that brought them closer. Five years later, they're still in love.

Their chats turned into phone calls and before long he wanted to meet her family. All of this before they even met each other in person. He would visit her family and offer to help with any tech issues at home. It was after his third consecutive visit with apples in hand (considered good etiquette back home), when her mother asked her if she was dating him. Turns out he would show up with one kilo of apples (about two lbs) every week and her mother was more concerned about the apples going bad as they couldn't finish them every week. Laila still jokes that he wooed her folks for permission to come visit her in Canada with just three kilos of apples.

When he went to visit, they made a deal that they would travel together for two weeks, and if by the end of it, they managed to survive, they're meant to be.

Needless to say, they had a wonderful time. And long story short, they lived to get married. Not once or twice but three times (to each other).

They are so blessed to call Canada their home. Their Canadian civil ceremony performed by me, was small by Indian standards, but she loved it. Both their families couldn't attend, but they had their Canadian families by their side, and they performed the Haldi ceremony – where bride and groom are prepped with turmeric paste and fragrances before the wedding. Nadiya, her Canadian mom, also did her henna herself at two am, the night before the wedding.

The Henna or Mehndi ceremony is customary in South Asian weddings to adorn the bride's palms and feet. Back in the day, the henna leaf was symbolic for a women's life. The leaf itself gets crushed to become a paste which then gives colour and fragrance to the person applying it. An ideal wife was supposed to be like that henna leaf, who sacrifices its own being to give meaning to her family's lives. In Laila's own words she said, "Edna was the perfect marriage commissioner. She was funny and thoughtful at the same time."

On the wedding day, her Canadian dad Nazim, walked her down the aisle. When Aziz said his vows, Laila chimed in to add that he would make her Chai Tea every morning, and he continues to do so years later.

Our Muslim wedding vows were meant to happen a year later with both our families present. In Western weddings, the bride is the center of attention. From families, to vendors, everyone must heed to the bride as it is her special day. In India, sadly the bride (and her family) whimsically does everything in their power to please the groom's family. Marriages are made in heaven but so are lightning and thunder. You see in their culture when you marry a man you marry his entire family.

Laila had a rollercoaster of weddings, and may have missed out on that 'one special day' exactly the way she wanted it, but in retrospect, she is so happy for their beautiful married life and everything that they have overcome together. I am most thankful to Laila for referring me to numerous other Muslim weddings and through that I have become good friends with her and Aziz.

Laila and Aziz.

Laos Custom and Traditions

A favourite tradition of mine is the Laos Wedding Ceremony. I was excited to be invited to their celebration. The day before. I was in awe of how the Laos community supported the couple in their traditional ceremony. From the elaborate dress code that had the women in colorful gorgeous silks and satins and the men in suits and dressy casual attire. There was an abundance of cultural and Canadian food for us to enjoy. Bob and I attended four Laos traditional ceremonies in which we were treated like royalty.

Once again we became like part of their family.

This cultural ceremony happened the day before I performed their marriage ceremony. The following is a description of what I observed during this colorful, exciting, and boisterous celebration, Danny so beautifully depicts for us. Traditional Laos Wedding Ceremonies are more spiritual than religious. The day is grand with lots of flower arrangements, everyone is dressed up in nice colours, and the day is one big party from when a person wakes up to whenever they pass out. The bride looks gorgeous wearing a traditional silk (Lao skirt), a silk blouse, and many jewelry items such as gold necklaces, bracelets, earrings, and bells. Her hair is tied up in a special way with sparkling golden decoration. The groom dresses up in a traditional silk sarong (Lao pants), a white silk shirt, and jewelry as well. Traditionally, Laos people often hold a Baci ceremony in the morning on the wedding date, and this is usually held at the bride's family. However, now many people omit this custom.

Traditionally, the groom will start their journey from his house or village. His family and friends will party the entire way to the bride's house or village. The groom is greeted at the door by the bride's family. This is where the bride's family tests the groom to see how hard he will fight to make it into the house to see his bride. This consists of a friendly feud between the two families. There is gift giving from the groom's family to the bride's family and a lot of cheering. Once the bride's family is happy with the groom's efforts, they open the doors and let him and his family in. Before he enters the house, a child in the family washes his feet and this represents washing the past away and starting a new beginning with his new family. The groom is then led into the house where the ceremony (the Baci), will take place. Her wedding party is there waiting, the groom and his wedding party take their seats, and then the bride is escorted in by a female family member.

The Baci is led by a Mor Phon (the master of ceremony). This person is usually an elder within the family or within the community. The center piece is decorated with lots of flowers and usually white flowers to represent purity. It is also surrounded by food, and this represents offerings to family members who are in the afterlife. Traditionally the ceremony is done at the bride's house and is on the ground while everyone gathers around them in a circle. It's started off with chanting by the Mor Phon, then the bride and groom get white strings tied around their wrists. The white strings are a blessing for good fortune and health. The Mor Phon ties the first strings, then the bride and grooms' parents, the elders, and then all the guests are welcome to participate. This is followed by some closing remarks by the Mor Phon. Then the bride and groom split a hard-boiled egg, and this represents fertility (this is our "you may kiss the bride"). After this the bride and groom are escorted to their bedroom by a female relative where the room, bed, and pillows are blessed. Once this is done the reception starts and everyone parties till dawn.

The ceremony base is the same, but everyone's families are different. Some parents like to have the ceremony done before noon and some like it done before supper. They had their traditional Laos ceremony done before noon and a lunch reception because they were also having their Canadian wedding the next day. The night before the wedding there is usually an Oun Dong (Rehearsal Dinner). Traditionally the bride's side has one and the groom's side has one at their family's place. This is usually a place for guests and out of town guests to come and hang out and say hi before the big day. They had their Laos Ceremony and Oun Dong on Friday and then they had their traditional wedding on Saturday.

The parents of one of the couples represented the Laos Community at my husband's Celebration of Life service. When they came up to me during the reception after the service, they asked, "Do you remember us?" "Well of course I do." I said. I was so touched that Bob and I meant so much to them that that they would make the effort and take the time to attend Bob's service. It was as if our extended family had joined us. They informed me that the other family members would have attended but they were away on vacation.

Bridesmaids with the groom.

The set up for a traditional Laos ceremony.

Danny and Vinni.

As much as we enjoyed other cultural traditions, we had traditions of our own that we enjoyed very much. We had all kinds of traditions for Christmas, Easter, Thanksgiving and Birthdays. The one that is heads and shoulders above all the rest is the Christmas Eve tradition.

A tradition that has lasted thirty-five years. Rod and Liz were dating, and Shawn was in university when we started the seafood Christmas Eve tradition.

For our first Christmas Eve tradition there were five of us, and in our last one, thirty-five years later, there were twenty-seven of us. When Shauntel and Sarah were little they embraced the seafood and Rosanne warned me if they grew up with expensive tastes it would be my fault. As the Grandchildren arrived and grew into teenagers they had fun initiating each of their partners as they joined us for their first Christmas Eve celebration not knowing what to expect. Besides our immediate family, our friends Paul and Gib became part of our family for many years, and my sister Flo joined us the last few years as well.

The menu had changed somewhat over the years, however, we did not deviate from the steak and lobster, or the aspic salad and the other dishes have become traditional.

It was the magic of the whole evening that everyone enjoyed so much. We would start at 3:00 p.m. with escargot and garlic bread. Then everyone but the food prep people would go for a walk in the park or a limo ride since Paul owned a limo business. We would get shrimp cocktail on the table, then would come the steak and lobster. After dinner each family member was given a tree ornament and they would tell us what were the important things that happened in their lives that year.

One year we had visitors from Venezuela, Shawn and Rosanne had an exchange student, so her father and brother came to spend Christmas with them. The highlight of the evening was when Santa and Mrs. Claus would arrive. The energy in the room went sky high. The last Christmas celebration for us was Christmas 2011. Thirty-five years reigned the end of an era. It was bittersweet, however, there comes a time in our lives when we must pass the torch on to the next generation to allow them to create their traditions, and we shall become their guests.

Bob preparing the lobster tails.

Traditional family Christmas Eve Dinner.

Sister Flo on Santa's knee (Joe) with Mrs. Claus (Bev).

Aboriginal Ceremony

One of my greatest honours as a marriage commissioner happened during a traditional aboriginal ceremony. I was asked by the Elder to walk with him and join him at the front of the venue. I was surprised as I was expecting to only be called forward to do my portion of the ceremony at the appropriate time. I stood there with great anticipation knowing that I was about to witness an inspirational and deeply meaningful aboriginal ceremony.

The wedding was all set to begin at 3:00 p.m. We arrived about twenty minutes to 3:00 p.m. There were a couple of people organizing and decorating the hall. Guests started arriving and the bride received a phone call the groom was just leaving Saskatoon. Which was over two hours away from Regina.

They asked us if we wanted to leave and come back in a couple of hours, but my husband and I decided since we had no other plans that we would stay. We watched how everybody went about the preparation in such a nice and easy manner, no one was rushing about all upset including the bride. It was wonderful to watch. The bride invited us to join them for the reception and supper. Throughout my experiences performing marriage ceremonies in various different cultures, we got to enjoy the different traditions and agreed to stay for the reception.

The groom arrived after two hours with the Elder.

A friend did the opening remarks and blessed the marriage in prayer. He then called on the Elder to take the service. It is an extremely touching ceremony. It was the first time I experienced smudging which I found to be a powerful spiritual ritual. Smudging is performed to remove negative energy as well as for centering and healing. The reason for smudging is it connects people to the Creator and provides communities with a way to gain spiritual protection and blessings, as well as to improve spiritual health. The smoke created by burning grass and sacred herbs is thought to purify the body and soul and bring clarity to the mind. I loved this part of the ceremony. I took the liberty to combine the elders' words in conjunction with a written ceremony I found on the internet.

"You who come now to join in marriage. Grant that

they give their sacred words to each other in the strength of your love. Enable them to grow in love and peace with you and with one another for all their days. The Elder then proceeded to perform the smudging ceremony. The Elder speaks to the couple as the smudging is performed "Oh, great Spirit bring the blessings of the East, South, West, and North. Mother Earth Father Sky, Creator of our souls within smudging."

As the elder smudges the bride and groom, he blesses them by saying, "May your hands be cleansed, that they create beautiful things. May your feet be cleansed, that they might take you where you most need to be. May your heart be cleansed, that you might hear its messages clearly. May your throat be cleansed, that you might speak rightly when words are needed. May your eyes be cleansed, that you might see the signs and wonders of the world. May this person and space be washed clean by the smoke of these fragrant plants and may that same smoke carry our prayers spiraling to the heavens. In honor of the bride and groom I cleanse them of all negativities. I banish away all those who would harm them, and I send away all negative thoughts, let this couple be filled with love and light from this day forward. Great Spirit above please protect the ones we love. We honor all you created as these two pledge their hearts and lives together. We honor Mother Earth and ask for their marriage to be abundant and grow stronger through the seasons. We honor fire and ask that their union be warm and glowing with love in their hearts. We honor wind and ask that they sail through life safe and calm, as in our father's arms. We honor water to clean and soothe their relationship that it may never thirst for love. With all the forces of the universe you created, we pray for harmony and true happiness as the bride and groom grow forever young together in marriage. Amen." Or "Aho."

I was called upon to do my part of the service. I started by saying a few words about love and commitment to each other. I then performed their marriage and ring vows and did a reading that they had requested. I also recognized each of their children in this marriage.

The friend closed the ceremony with a prayer. I was so delighted to be part of this aboriginal custom. After the ceremony was over my husband and I were asked to sit at the table with the Bride and Groom and the Elder. A delicious dinner of all kinds of wild meat, elk, deer, and moose, along with rabbit stew and delicious chocolate cake for dessert was served.

The groom presented a gift to me of an 8-inch round stick with five different colored ribbons and a feather.

The beaded white feather means nurturing friendship.

The yellow ribbon means peace.

The green ribbon means endurance.

The red ribbon means healing.

The pink ribbons mean direction in life.

The white ribbon means harmony.

I was so touched by this gift that I have always had it in my office at the top of my desk where I could see it every day. What a beautiful, enjoyable experience it was to me.

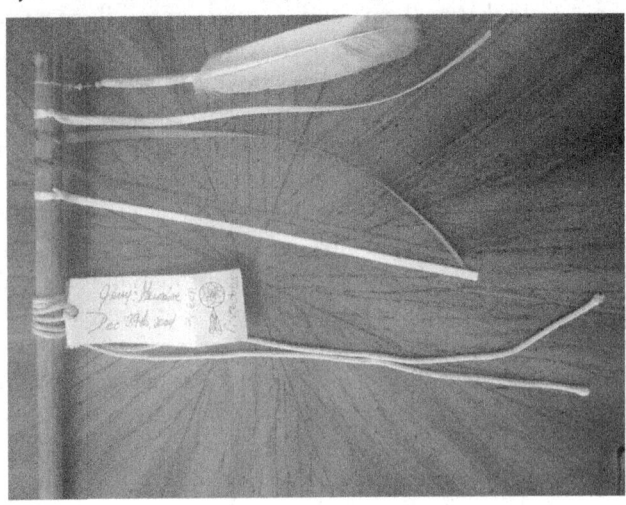

CHAPTER 8:
GOING THAT EXTRA MILE

I have performed many multicultural marriages. Below is a love story of one of the most memorable and the hoops they had to go through to be together.

Karen and Dave met in January of 2001. Karen's first language is Spanish, and she knew little English at the time. Dave's first language is English, and he did not know any Spanish at the time. They first communicated through smiles, drawings, and the help of a bilingual Spanish-English dictionary that Karen carried with her everywhere she went. This is their fairy tale love story.

Dave was born in BC and moved to Saskatchewan with his parents at the age of ten. Karen was born and raised in Venezuela. She was a teacher who decided to take a semester off to learn English abroad. A few days before her twenty-second birthday, Karen arrived in the middle of a blizzard and saw snow for the first time. She had planned to go back home at the end of the program and return to work, which she did. However, she had no plan to fall in love. There was instant chemistry when they met, and attraction followed by time spent together on dates shortly after their meeting. After the program ended, Karen went back home, hoping the relationship would continue, but it was uncertain it would happen. Dave promised he would visit, and they would continue. According to him, he had met "the one." He learned some Spanish in preparation for his trip. It was his first-time meeting Karen's family in person. Five months flew by, and on his second visit to Venezuela, he could hold a basic Spanish conversation. He culminated his trip with the dramatic 'down on one knee' marriage proposal and asking Karen's parents for their permission to marry her. Their relationship evolved to a permanent commitment to each other.

In 2003 Karen travelled to Canada with her parents. She officially married Dave in a small, civil wedding ceremony. In attendance were their parents and the close friends they had met during their time dating while Karen was studying in Canada. One of those friends is my granddaughter Shauntel, who became Karen's closest friend and was the maid of honour when I officiated at their ceremony. A week later, Karen returned home, and Dave remained in Canada. Dave applied to sponsor Karen, but it was a lengthy process that took more than time and patience; it was not easy. They spent most of their time on telephone conversations where they talked about their goals, the family they would create, and their commitment. In 2004 the couple married once again in a Catholic wedding in Venezuela attended by Karen's large family and many friends.

A couple of years went by, and in January 2006, after having an emotional farewell by her family, friends, colleagues, and students, Karen moved to Canada. However, after Karen's arrival, due to misinformation from different immigration officers (each one they talked to would give a different answer), they had to start the process all over. It was a lot of paperwork. Karen could stay legally in the country, but only as a visitor. Karen could not work or even obtain a library card to get books, so she had to depend on Dave even to read. Karen would give Dave the names of books to bring home and would spend many days inside the apartment reading. Dave was attending university during the day and working nights and weekends. The few friends Karen had, were also busy working. It was winter, so she would only go out for walks around the block each day to get some fresh air. International phone calls were expensive, so calling home anytime was not a possibility. They were saving every penny. They had to pay thousands of dollars through the entire process. There was frustration, but they were unwilling to separate again.

Through friends, she knew of opportunities to volunteer to help new immigrants. Shauntel's mom, an elementary school teacher, allowed Karen to volunteer in her classroom. Shortly after, Karen was volunteering in almost every classroom at the school. At the same time, she was volunteering at the Immigrant Women Centre (IWC), assisting in the ESL classes and the church.

A year later, Karen obtained permanent residency and could work, but not yet as a schoolteacher, so she started the accreditation process. She continued volunteering and enjoyed it, but she needed an income. The immigration and accreditation process were expensive. She had to work different part-time jobs. The IWC offered her the position as the primary instructor for the class, and she took a job at a clothing department store and then at the Rider store. Another year went by, and Karen received the confirmation of her accreditation and could go back to teaching in schools.

Fast forward twenty years since they started dating, Karen and Dave have a wonderful marriage raising their two incredible children in their multicultural home.

Karen and Dave.

I appreciate when people go that extra mile to be together or to do something special for a loved one. This reminds me of the day my husband Bob retired. It was important for me to make his day special and memorable. Bob retired from the transit in 1987 due to health issues. He used to say, "So and so retired today," and I would ask, "What did they do for him?" He said, "Nothing, he just got off the bus and walked to his car and left after thirty-five years."

That bothered me. Since at SGI we celebrated birthdays and retirements and when people would leave our department. I thought that is not going to happen to Bob. I had the boys make a sign large enough to fit the back window of the bus saying "The Last Run, thirty-three years." I invited all my family and some friends to meet at the transit barns and notified the media. A reporter got on his bus earlier in the day and interviewed Bob. He didn't think anything of it.

When Bob came to the bus stop at the transit barns, he was shocked to see over thirty of us get on the bus for the last half of his final run. He had no idea. He said he became as nervous as his first day of work. Since then, the union have been doing a recognition on the retirees last day.

I started a tradition that was long overdue.

Bob's last run.

CHAPTER 9: SAME-SEX MARRIAGES

On November 5, 2004, it was ruled that the common-law opposite-sex definition of marriage violated the equality rights of same-sex couples. Same-sex marriage became law in Saskatchewan on this date, and marriage became the lawful union of two persons to the exclusion of all others.

All marriage commissioners in Saskatchewan, received a letter from the Department of Justice indicating that we must perform same-sex marriages, or we must resign.

I was enjoying my retirement profession as a marriage commissioner and did not want to resign. Therefore, I made a conscious decision to perform same-sex marriages.

To date I have performed eighteen same-sex ceremonies. Twelve female couples and six male couples.

I performed my first same-sex marriage on November 24, 2004 approximately three weeks after same-sex marriages became law.

Two women from a small town in Saskatchewan. There were about thirty people in attendance, and they were so nervous as they did not know what to expect, all they knew was they wanted to get married.

I was nervous as well since the terminology was different. Instead of husband and wife, the word spouse was to be used. Instead of, "I pronounce you husband and wife," the words used were, "To be married."

I didn't notice or feel any difference in energy at this ceremony. However, when I performed the first male couple in the spring of 2005 there was about ninety invited guests. When I entered the venue, you could feel the chill in the room it felt like ice. I proceeded with my ceremony. At the beginning of each service, I always start my service with "To the parents of the bride and groom, this is a special day in your lives as well." By 2005 I had already done almost 1,000 weddings that rolled off my tongue naturally. Instead of saying to the parents of the couple, I said to the parents of the bride and groom. Everybody laughed, and the couple in front of me almost doubled over in laugher. I did not realize just what I had said that was so funny.

After the ceremony an elderly gentleman sitting in the front row called me over and introduced himself as one of the Groom's father. He said, "Thank you so much for warming up the place by your unintentional comment. I felt that broke the ice." He too felt the chill in the room.

I performed a ceremony for two men who had asked another marriage commissioner to perform their ceremony for them, but he refused because of his religious beliefs. They were daunted by his refusal and took him to court. The marriage commissioner lost the case since we could not discriminate. Shortly after gay marriages were legalized, I married two women, one American and the other Canadian. They got married in Regina at the Band Stand. It was a small intimate wedding with just family members and a few close friends present. The father of the Regina woman was bothered by this grey-haired stranger who took pictures of the couple when I allowed a photo op.

He proceeded to follow this stranger to find out exactly why he was there after the ceremony was over and the people were leaving. When we met up after the ceremony, my husband Bob, assisted me in taking my robe off and placing it in the bag. The Father said, "Oh that's who you belong to, I was wondering who this stranger was taking pictures of MY daughter." The father appeared concerned about what this stranger was going to do with these photos and who would see them, the stigma was still there regarding same-sex marriage.

I noticed that the stigma was prevalent more so with elderly men, coming to terms with this new law. In my experience, women seemed to be more acceptable and open to the changes. Having grown up in an era where gays and lesbians were not even mentioned, my husband found it difficult to accept. Even more so with male couples than with female couples. In the beginning, he even had a problem taking their picture during a photo op. Bob would always answer the door for my interviews so he could meet the couple up front. When the first male couple rang the doorbell for our interview, he wouldn't get out of his chair to answer the door. I asked him afterward why he wouldn't answer the door since that was what he always did, he said, "I didn't want to."

However, he did get a change of attitude as time went on. He used to run into the one male couple while grocery shopping and they were always so friendly and funny toward him. He would come home and share with me their conversations and he got a more favorable view of male same-sex couples.

Two east Indian women one from Florida and the other from Regina were married in the strictest of secrecy. They will never divulge to their families that they are married since it is the biggest sin in India and against the law.

Another East Indian couple had their marriage arrangements complete and two nights before their marriage ceremony the family in India found out and demanded their daughter return home to India immediately. The marriage never happened.

Two women wanted to marry in Louisiana, USA, who both worked for Law Enforcement. Since same-sex marriages were illegal in that state, their boss advised them if they got married in another jurisdiction like Canada, they would recognize them as a married couple. They chose

Regina since the route included the states they wanted to visit. Also, we had the Royal Canadian Mounted Police Depot which is our Canadian national police force. The main training center in Canada for cadets is here in Regina. They were excited to experience the cadets in training and see our beautiful facility here in the Queen city.

They arrived here in Regina, eager to get married and I happily obliged. The ceremony was to take place at the Band Stand. Marriage commissioners and wedding cars had permission to drive through the park to get to the Band Stand.

While we were waiting, we noticed a fellow just staring at us and on the phone loudly complaining that we had driven through the park and were parked at the band stand. Soon two city police officers arrived on the scene. We explained the situation, that wedding cars and marriage commissioners had permission and that I was performing a wedding for a same-sex couple shortly.

The officers went to the entrance and stopped the couple from entering even though they knew the rules that they could drive into the park. They had to park their car on the street and walk in. I was angry with the gentlemen for being so aggressive in his speech when discussing the matter with the city police. I was also disgusted with the officers for stopping the couple from entering the park with their vehicle and having to walk in. It was disheartening to have this kind of discrimination take place in the city that I have advocated, promoted, and supported all these years. I felt bad because I did not want this to be a reflection on me.

Upon their arrival we proceeded with their ceremony. Cheryl was fifty-two and Rachel was twenty. I never saw so much love in a bride's eyes as in Rachel's eyes when she was saying her vows to her partner. I became Facebook friends with Cheryl. She invited us to come to New Orleans and they would show us around. The year we were thinking of planning to go Katrina hit New Orleans, and since it took so long to get things in order there it never happened. I reached out to Rachel to let her know that I was writing a book about my experiences as a marriage commissioner, and I wanted to add her and Cheryl's unique love story. Rachel shared with me the deep love and caring that they had for each other even though there was such a big age difference. The age difference never effected their lifestyle or their love for one another.

Cheryl and Rachel met at work in 2000. She was a Corporal in Criminal Patrol with the local Sheriff's Office and Rachel was a 9-1-1 dispatcher. She was transferred into dispatch (due to a medical issue), and Rachel had recently wrecked her car and needed a ride. Cheryl offered to drop Rachel off and pick her up when needed. They started talking a lot. Cheryl made Rachel laugh; Rachel made Cheryl smile. They started dating in 2001. Cheryl worked the "swing shift" 12 a.m. to 12 p.m. Rachel was on the night shift the next day (6:00 p.m. to 6:00 a.m.) Cheryl called and asked if Rachel was hungry because she was going to stop at Waffle house (a chain of twenty-four-hour diners popular in the South). She asked if Rachel wanted to meet her there. Rachel said yes, hung up the phone, changed outfits five times and went to meet her future wife for their first "date" (this happened in May of 2001). They ended up talking for almost two hours at the restaurant. They quickly became inseparable. It was a little rough at first, Rachel was not out.

She had always known that she was different and that she liked women as well as men, that to her gender didn't matter. She just had never found a reason to tell her family. Her family is from Southeastern Louisiana, and pretty much everyone is Catholic. She was raised in the Church but had stopped going due to her sexuality and the way the Catholic Church viewed her because of it. Cheryl was thirty-two years older than her and had been out for a while. Everyone at work said Cheryl was the youngest fifty something they knew, and Rachel was the oldest twenty something they knew, so they met somewhere in the middle. That was so true. They clicked, their hearts knew each other, their souls spoke, all the clichés felt perfect for them. Rachel came out to her family, and it was a little rocky, but she never lost contact or love with them. They moved in together at the end of 2001. They went about their lives together. They loved to travel and tried to do small weekend trips throughout the year, but also a "big" vacation once a year. They were that couple that people teased about being "so in love." Cheryl retired in 2003, but still did some volunteer things. Rachel was full-time by then at a local Police Department as a 9-1-1 Dispatcher. In 2004, Cheryl's Mom passed away from breast cancer, after that Cheryl told Rachel she wanted to get married. Rachel laughed and told her it wasn't legal. Cheryl said it is in Canada. Rachel didn't think they'd let them do that since they didn't live there. Cheryl (hard-headed, stubborn woman) set out to prove Rachel wrong. She looked online, called a couple of government agencies, and she was right, they would let them. Rachel said that's all well and good, but she never asked her if she wanted to. Cheryl got down on her knee at the end of the bed and told Rachel she wanted to spend the rest of her life with her, that she was her heart, that she made the days' worth it. They both cried, Rachel said yes, and they decided to go to Canada. They looked at all the different places they could go and made the decision to go to Regina Saskatchewan. Since the RCMP depot was there and they just loved the RCMP. Cheryl also loved Wyoming and Colorado, and that is where she wanted to take Rachel for their honeymoon. The pictures of Regina were beautiful. Rachel got the task of picking all the details for the wedding. She knew she wanted it to be outside, so she started looking for a park and found the Bandstand at Wascana center, which was so perfect. She then found a hotel, and a restaurant for their wedding dinner. She just needed a marriage commissioner, so, she pulled up a list which was in alphabetical order and started calling. She left message after message.

No one answered the phone. The first person who answered said they weren't available before she even told them the date. She waited a couple of days and received no phone calls back. She didn't know what to think or do. She pulled the list back up and called a few more, either no answers or voicemails. She stopped leaving messages and took another day to think and decided to give it one more try before telling Cheryl they might have to change plans. She called a couple and had the same response, no answer or voicemail. Then she called the next number not expecting much, and to her surprise she got an answer. She had to look down at the list to see who she had called, Ms. Edna McCall. A warm voice confirmed that's who she was talking to, and Rachel quickly launched into her story of being from the US and wanting to get married in Canada due to the recent change in laws. Rachel said, "Ms. Edna was kind, sweet, and attentive. She asked questions but made her feel so comfortable." She had a date and a plan. They drove for two days to get there and had the best time. They stopped in South Dakota on the side of the road to watch a field full of lightning bugs and held hands. They drove a second day and crossed into Canada, when they got to the border, the border agent was so excited that they were "coming to take advantage of Canada's great laws," and arrived in Regina in the evening. They met with me on their first full day in Regina and felt we made them feel so welcome. They always called us Ms. Edna and Mr. Bob. Everything was set. Rachel's Mom and brother met them in Regina the day before. In Rachel's words, "The wedding was beautiful. Every moment was a dream come true." They left a couple of days later and honeymooned for two weeks traveling through Wyoming, Colorado, and New Mexico. They settled into "married life." They had already been living together for four years at that time, truly not too much changed. They just settled into each other even more, knowing that both of them looked at this as a forever thing.

Cheryl retired before they got married, and she loved to travel, go to the casino, go hiking, go camping, meet friends for dinner, have friends and family over, go to music concerts, the beach, and Rachel got to join her for all of these adventures. Everyone knew they were one of those married couples that enjoyed each other's company and did most things together. That's not to say they did everything together, but they were together and loved it more than when they were apart, other than Rachel still having to work full time as a 9-1-1 dispatcher. They had five more blissful years after they got married, being together, traveling, enjoying life and each other. They weren't perfect, but they worked together to make each other happy. In 2010 Cheryl slowed down a bit, which was unusual. She could run circles around her up to that point, it didn't matter that she was thirty-something years older.

Cheryl was so full of life, energy, joie de vivre, spirit, whatever you want to call it, she had it. That's why they didn't hesitate to contact a doctor. Much to their chagrin Cheryl was diagnosed with a severe type of cancer. She went through rigorous cancer treatments and all the while Rachel loved and supported her through every treatment, her down days, and all the medical assistance that she was able to handle. She stood by her side day after day for over two years until the diagnosis became terminal.

On Cheryl's last night she woke up around 2:00 a.m. Rachel was in a chair next to her bed, holding her hand. Rachel got into the bed with her and told her that she would be ok, that she loved her more than words, and that it was okay for her to go. Cheryl opened her eyes and reached her head toward her. She bent over and she kissed her forehead. Rachel just held her as she took her last breaths around 4:00 a.m. Her love was no longer on this Earth. Cheryl passed away on January 27, 2013. They had been together for twelve years. Rachel had her cremated as were her wishes and had a memorial service about a month after she passed. What I found so poignant about Rachel and Cheryl's story is how they had to confront the dogma of the law of the State, the Catholic Church, and the acceptance of her family. The conviction that they shared shows that love conquers all.

Rachel has since met a wonderful man and remarried in 2018. She feels truly blessed that he loves her, and she loves him, and a part of her will always be in love with Cheryl. Rachel hasn't moved on without her. As she said to me, "I am who I am because of our time together, Cheryl will always be in my heart and soul."

Cheryl and Rachel.

EDNA I. MCCALL

CHAPTER 10: MEMORABLE CELEBRATIONS

Bob and I were both avid volunteers in our community. One organization that was near and dear to our hearts was the *Play it Safe* program sponsored by SGI. The most important weekend in Saskatchewan is Labour Day weekend. On this weekend, the Saskatchewan Roughriders meet their biggest rival, the Winnipeg Blue Bombers. The city is a sea of green as fans dress up and mingle everywhere to get pumped up for the big game. The Blue Bombers were staying at the Regina Inn (now known as The Double Tree Hilton) along with a large contingency of their fans from Winnipeg.

One particular labour day weekend, Bob and I volunteered on Saturday morning to wrap hotdogs for the *Play It Safe* day. This is an opportunity for fans to meet the football players out on the field, mingle and meet their favourite players. They got their photos taken with them as many families brought their children for this special day. After Bob and I spent the morning wrapping hot dogs, we came home smelling like one. We had to clean up quickly, as I had a wedding ceremony to perform within the hour at our place.

A Dr. and her manager from Williston, North Dakota decided to come to Regina to get married, they made arrangements with me to get married in my home. They made reservations at The Regina Inn to spend a nice quiet weekend there, a mini honeymoon so to speak. When they came to my place for the marriage ceremony, they were annoyed with what was going on at this celebration that involved so many guests at the hotel. They couldn't sleep, they had to put up with the noise all day and night. When they complained, they did not get an apology, they were just told that this is a big event and nothing was done to stop the partying. They stayed for quite some time at my place enjoying the peace and quiet of our home. In retrospect, the Blue Bombers probably won thus all the celebrating.

In 1967, Canada was to celebrate its 100th birthday. The City of Regina established the Centennial Committee to develop special programs and projects to celebrate the milestone. They decided to create a city-wide summer celebration, ending with a summer fair. In honour of Saskatchewan pioneers, the celebration was named Buffalo Days, which it was known as for forty-two years until it was re-named Queen City Ex in 2009.

It was during Buffalo Days that I had the privilege to perform a wedding at the Scarth Street Mall in downtown Regina. Doug Swayne and Roxene Harris had met on the costume committee and spent so much time together that eventually love blossomed.

They decided what better time to get married than during Buffalo Days. The wedding was advertised in local media. I obliged the couples request to help make their day special by going in costume as well.

The day of the wedding, arrangements were made to have a double-decker bus pick up the wedding party, relatives and friends. Bob and I were asked to meet there as well. The groom was escorted on the bus to the top level. After all the guests were on the bus, the bride was ushered in where the groom couldn't see her.

We proceeded downtown to the Scarth Street Mall on 11th avenue. I had the pleasure of leading the procession down the crowded mall as the Dreher band played. We continued to the designated spot with the groom in front and the bride at the back, I started with, "Here comes the bride," as she made her way through the crowd to the front to stand beside the groom who saw his beautiful bride for the first time that day.

I looked around, I couldn't believe the mall was packed with people, the largest crowd of uninvited guests that I had experienced to date. Everyone came to see the wedding and were attentive during the ceremony. The crowd went wild when I said, "You may now kiss your bride." When the ceremony concluded the band started playing, the bride and groom danced their first dance much to the delight of the crowd who cheered them on. I was honoured to have been asked because I do love excitement, crowds, performers, and acting, and this wedding incorporated all of the above. The crowd cheered as we leisurely walked to Victoria Park across the street for pictures. That was the first time I did not wear my robe.

Fast forward, I recently met with a couple to plan their ceremony. At the end of the meeting the groom said, "Edna, you and I have been down this road before," I asked him what he meant by that. He said, you married me and Roxene during Buffalo Days. My mouth dropped open as he shared that because I distinctively remember performing that memorable ceremony on Scarth Street Mall.

Unfortunately, Roxene passed away in 2018 and Doug has now found a new love Claudine Laurent. I had the pleasure of performing their marriage ceremony just recently. I was delighted to witness and participate in another love story.

The crowd on Scarth Street.

The first dance.

The Buffalo Day wedding.

My two-thousandth marriage ceremony that I performed was held on a leap year February 29, 2020, just before covid hit. It was held at the Hotel Saskatchewan in the Royal Suite where the Queen and Prince Philip would stay when they visited Regina on a number of occasions. The bedroom was huge, and the main area was a large area with soft seating placed around the room. There was a large table in the dining room laden with a wide variety of delicious food with the most gorgeous presentation. It was fit for a Queen. I began the ceremony by announcing that I was performing my two-thousandth ceremony. The guests cheered and applauded my milestone wedding. Bob and I were delighted to stay for a short while and enjoy the refreshments and delicious food set out for the reception. I was proud to have accomplished this milestone in my twenty-fifth year as a marriage commissioner.

Another significant date where I married four couples was 08/08/08 which was the eighth day of the eighth month of the year 2008. However, the first couple that I performed the marriage ceremony for went one better. They got married at 8:00 a.m. on the eight of the eight month 2008, 08/08/08/08. As we gathered at the house, it was five minutes to 8:00 and the groom's mother had not yet arrived. There were a few anxious moments until one minute to 8:00 around the corner of the house she came. I proceeded with the ceremony at 8:00 a.m., that was the earliest that I had ever done a ceremony. The other weddings went off without a hitch. As usual, Bob got me to where I needed to go on time for the remainder of the weddings.

Curtis Kopciuch and Heather Hampton exchanged wedding vows on Canada Day during a beautiful garden ceremony in White City. It was true to a Canada Day wedding right down to the red and white bridal sneakers which was the best kept secret of the day as they were hidden under the bride's wedding dress.

In sharing their story for their wedding plans with me and their love for Canada Day at our meeting, they wanted to use the Canada Day theme. I totally supported their idea since I love when people use their imagination to come up with something unique. This is why I love being a marriage commissioner because of the diversification of ideas, mine, and theirs. Canada Day has always been a big day for Curtis. He loves being a Canadian. One year he dressed up as Captain Canada and wandered around Calgary in a goofy Canada hat, red shorts, and red shoes with a flag for a cape. He sure got a lot of attention with horns honking at him.

When they were discussing their wedding, Curtis came up with the idea to do a Canada Day theme. He is a proud Canadian and always loved hockey so there was nothing better than to have this theme on his special day and to get married on July 1. It didn't take much imagination to combine his three great loves – Jennifer, being Canadian, and hockey. But it took a bit of convincing before Jennifer agreed to marry her man in a hockey jersey.

However, she agreed since Curtis was patriotic and he wanted the wedding to be memorable. He picked the day since Canada Day is a holiday, so they will always have the day off, and red is his favorite color and he wanted to wear a hockey jersey. Jennifer explained that Team Canada jerseys were a safe bet since Curtis is a Montreal Canadian fan and she cheers for the Canucks. They did not want a formal froufrou wedding.

As part of the Canada Day theme the groom along with his five groomsmen donned the red, black, and white jerseys complete with their names and numbers. The five bridesmaids wore red dresses with black boas and black shoes. Jennifer had maple leaf tattoos on her body and had maple leaves on her white wedding dress and of course her red and white sneakers. When I arrived at the venue I was so amazed at how great everyone looked, including the guests in their Canada Day attire. I was excited when I saw the wedding party all dressed in red and white.

During the ceremony, I reminded the young couple that to mark their anniversary each year, and as a symbol of their love, they were to give each other a single red rose. Something the couple agreed to do to mark a significant day in their lives.

Even family and friends got into the spirit of the Canada Day theme by wearing maple leaf ties and red and white attire. Everything at the hall was decorated in red and white. Pizza and beer were served to the guests at the wedding reception.

According to Curtis. Everyone loves pizza and both pizza and beer went with the hockey theme. As for the wedding cake they had individual white cupcakes with red maple leaf sprinkles.

Curtis and Jennifer wanted it to be one big Canada Day party something for everyone to remember. It was a blast of a Canada Day Celebration. To this day they celebrate their anniversary on their favorite day.

July 1, Canada Day wedding.

A unique situation that I came across was on December 31, 1999. According to the Marriage Act of Saskatchewan, the hours for solemnizing a marriage are between 6:00 a.m. and 10:00 p.m. However, there was an exception made only for the date of December 31, 1999 as this was a novel circumstance. On this date a marriage may be solemnized any time i.e., on the stroke of midnight.

Bob and I headed out to White City leaving home around 11:00 p.m. It was an exciting night for us to experience the turn of the century together. I started the ceremony at 11:45 p.m. There was a lot of anticipation about when we should start the actual ceremony. We timed it so when it came to the vows, the Groom said his vows in the closing minutes of 1999. At midnight we all acknowledged the turning of the century and then the bride said her vows in the opening minutes of 2000, a millennium apart. Initially, the couple wanted to be married at the stroke of midnight, I suggested they do it this way. The vows they spoke to one another may have been a thousand years apart, yet their hearts were joined in mere minutes. We were invited to stay for a beautiful feast of seafood and steak and everything in between. It was a magical way to begin a new century.

Another New Year's Eve ceremony I performed was at Mosaic Stadium. This was truly a New Year's Eve party; everyone was dressed to the nines. You could feel the excitement in the air. We proceeded with the ceremony on a real high, Graham and Alicia chose to incorporate the Unity Canvas Painting Ceremony:

The ceremony lets the couple celebrate their ceremony in an artistic way that truly represents themselves. Here are the words I spoke as the couple painted their canvas.

"Every marriage starts out as a blank canvas, a new beginning. The couple has chosen colored paint to represent the experiences that lie ahead – the milestones, challenges, dreams, and celebrations are the moments that become the days that make up the years of their marriage."

There will be places on the canvas when the colors blend and mix, flowing together, creating a new color of experiences shared.

There will be places when the colors stay separate and stand out alone and independently, and there may be places of contrast. Parts of the canvas that look dark or messy and not at all to the couples liking. While another spot remains blank and bare.

However, when you step back and look at the canvas in its entirety, you will see that it clearly is "An Original Masterpiece" unlike anything you've seen before. This was such a unique addition to the ceremony that they had chosen to do. I was so proud to participate in it.

We were invited to stay for the reception. It was definitely a special New Year's Eve party. The bride and groom sat at a small, raised stage just the two of them which was elegantly decorated with lights and drapery.

There were food stations all around the hall. A carving station of Kobe beef, sliders, crab and lobster, chicken and beef, sushi and shrimp, salad bar, martini mash potato bar, Austrian schnitzel (in honor of Grampa) and a huge double-decker dessert table laden with an array of mini cakes, chocolate covered strawberries, and every kind of dainty you can think of. After visiting all the food stations with a gap in between, I finished off with a dessert of various kinds. I heard afterwards there was a potato table with ten different kinds of toppings that I had missed. I could not let that pass me by, so off I went to the potato bar ending the evening with potatoes and several kinds of toppings.

Vow Renewals

When I received my first request to perform a vow renewal for a couple, I did not know what to think. I was unsure of what I would say. Upon reflection, I determined to have them tell me their life story of how they met, when they got married, and why they wanted to renew their vows. This would allow me to create a personal and touching ceremony directly related to their experiences and love for one another over the years. A marriage ceremony is the beginning of a couple's life together, but vow renewals are a reflection of their life and experiences. It is a celebration of what they have already been through together and a deepening of their commitment to be together for the rest of their life. Sometimes new rings were exchanged, or they had their rings rededicated once again. The reason for choosing to have a vow renewal varies with the couples. A common choice made for how many years they were married. Anywhere from ten, twenty-five, fifty, sixty years and anything in between. Sometimes a couple was married in another country and all they did was sign papers at city hall without a ceremony. By renewing their vows, here in Canada, they were able to have a ceremony and the brides were given an opportunity to wear the wedding dress of their dreams. As of today, I have performed twenty-one vow renewals.

Rowena's Story

I would like to share a touching story of a couple that

shared with me their story of twenty-five years of marriage and what wowed them most about each other. Dwayne and Rowena went to the same high school. Dwayne was known for having fun, so Rowena thought he would be a good person to ask to be her grad escort. Before grad they got together at a cabaret, to this day they argue about the date of the cabaret and who picked who up.

They got engaged on December 12, 1981. Dwayne took Rowena out for a romantic supper at The Keg and then they went for a drive through Wascana park. They parked overlooking the lake and he proposed. They got married on July 3, 1982, at St. Joseph's church in Balgonie and had the reception in Pilot Butte.

One and a half years later they were blessed with the birth of their daughter, Brandy, and two and a half years after that they were blessed with the birth of their son, Josh. They relocated to McLean in 1984 where they live to this day.

Dwayne has a romantic side and has shown this many times, but there were two times that were especially touching and memorable. For their tenth anniversary, Dwayne secretly planned a weekend getaway to Edmonton. The night before they left he had a game show rehearsed with the kids. Dwayne was the game show host and Rowena and Brandy and Josh were the contestants. Dwayne would ask a question and the kids would get the answers wrong but Rowena would get them right. After the game show was over, he told Rowena that she was the winner and had won a weekend getaway to the Fantasyland Hotel in the West Edmonton Mall, and that they were leaving the next day. He had booked her off work and had arranged for her parents to look after the kids.

Just this past December, Dwayne once again swept her off her feet. December 12th was the twenty-fifth anniversary of the day he asked her to marry him. He sent twenty-five roses to her at work. Work had been so crazy busy she didn't even realize it was the twelfth. As soon as she saw the roses she realized what day it was and hadn't planned anything. She called Dwayne to thank him for the roses and told him she would take him out for supper, where ever he wanted to go.

When he picked her up after work, she asked him if he had decided where he wanted to go for supper. He said he hadn't decided yet. Next thing she knows, they are pulling into the parking lot at the Regina Inn (the hotel where they had spent their wedding night).

Dwayne had once again totally surprised her. He had booked in at the hotel and had made supper reservations at The Diplomat. He had packed her clothes (which included a couple of dresses, slip, pantyhose, shoes he even remembered to find, the belt that went with one dress, all her makeup, curling iron and everything else she needed). He also packed wine, wine glasses and candles.

Needless to say, it was a special night which she could fully enjoy because he had also made arrangements for her to have the next day off work. These have been twenty-five wonderful years that she has spent with her best friend and love of her life.

Dwayne's Story

They have been married for the past twenty-five years, but it's been the last seven years that have meant the most to Dwayne. This is where he learned the true meaning of the word "Love." Dwayne found out it's easy to love someone when things are going well. But the true meaning is to love that person when things are bad.

In today's times of the, I need it now, I want it now or I'm gone, he is grateful knowing he found someone who loves him no matter what the world throws at them and he knows she'll be there. The past seven years have been rough for them because of health issues. Rowena could've bailed a long time ago but she didn't, she showed the true meaning of the vows "in sickness and in health," they took twenty-five years ago. Dwayne said, "So Edna, this is what has wowed me about Rowena, showing me the true meaning of the word 'love.'"

I remember feeling emotional during their vow renewal as I shared their love story with the guests who were also emotional. It is the couple's reflection of their life together and the hardships they have overcome that makes performing vow renewals meaningful and touching for me. It gives me great pleasure to be a part of a couple's desire to the recommitment to love.

CHAPTER 11:
ODDBALL WEDDINGS

Throughout my years as a marriage commissioner, I have been asked to perform ceremonies in some of the most odd, strange, surprising, and beautiful places as well as experiencing some odd, strange, surprising, and shocking behaviours.

One particular couple informed me that they were planning a theme wedding. At first, I thought it sounded like fun because I love to dress up to play the part. The photo of my costume looked good, but it turned out to be ill-fitting and I looked ridiculous. There were special costumes ordered for the wedding party as well.

However, an upset bride's dress was so ill-fitting that she had to rush out and purchase another wedding dress. Had I known that the bride was not going to wear her costume I would have worn my robe instead which I feel comfortable in. The reason for the request is because they were avid Harry Potter fans. I was happy to oblige their request. The complete service was written by the bride which I thought was fitting. I felt good about presenting what she contributed to the ceremony, and I added the legal jargon to make it official. After the service, I rushed into the bathroom because I couldn't wait to get out of that ridiculous getup. I handed it back to the bride for her keeping and advised her I would not be needing this again since my Harry Potter days are officially over.

Edna in a Harry Potter costume.

To continue with some of my oddball experiences, I have performed three ceremonies on Halloween, October 31. I felt weird as I was looking at all these cats in the audience ready to yell Tricks or Treats. This was in my first year as a marriage commissioner. Each guest was given a cat mask. The bride wore a beautiful wedding dress, and the groom wore a tuxedo. I found it strange that they were dressed in elaborate wedding attire and the invited guests were cats. It was a bit nerve racking to deliver the ceremony to a sea of cats. As soon as I introduced the couple, the meowing started immediately. Trick or treat.

Another Halloween wedding was at the Conexus Art Centre with a large number of invited guests, all dressed in costume. It was exciting since everyone was trying to guess who I was. I was asked to wear a mask as well. Oh, the things I won't do at the request of my couples. I was struggling with this mask as it kept moving down and I couldn't see what I was reading. I was close to ripping that mask off my face but endured and managed to get through it.

Medieval wedding. Over the years I have performed three ceremonies with the medieval custom included. At this particular wedding, I was asked to dress in costume. This was the first time I was asked to wear something besides my robe. I refused. I did not yet have the confidence and felt uncomfortable doing this. I did however, compromise with the couple and said that I would wear a scarf that accessorized what the bride and groom were wearing over the top of my robe. The wedding party and guests were all dressed in costume. This was interesting for me to see how all the guests cooperated with them by bringing to life the vision that the couple desired. I performed the usual ceremony which was followed by the medieval custom.

The Medieval custom, which is the Jumping of the Broom, symbolizes the bride and groom cutting ties with their parents and the ties being swept away. At this time, the best man and Maid of Honor walked over to where the broom and sword were and picked them up, and placed them on the floor in front of the bride and groom.

The Bride and Groom jumped over the broom and sword, and I proceeded to read the following poem that describes the significance of this custom.

> *Dark and Stormy may come the weather,*
> *This man and woman are joined together,*
> *Let none but him that makes the thunder,*

Put this man and woman asunder,
I therefore announce you both the same,
Be good, go long, and keep up your name,
The broomstick's jumped, the world's not wide,
She's now your own, go kiss your bride.

To end this chapter, I wanted to share the most shocking and uncouth behavior of a bride that I ever witnessed. It was a small backyard wedding with family and friends for a middle-aged couple. When I came to the part of the ceremony where I said, "You may now seal your vows with a kiss, the groom decided to get passionate. As he leaned in to kiss her, he slipped her the tongue. The bride immediately pulled away slapped his face and yelled "you pig" I darn near died right there. I don't know what happened after that, I never heard.

CHAPTER 12:
BIKER WEDDING

You can say I am a wild child. I was born to be wild. I would jump at any chance I had to plop my butt on the back of a motorcycle. I never drove one but if I heard the rumble of a Harley coming down the street I would find some way to get a ride. If I heard that the groom was making his entrance to the venue on his motorbike, you can bet your sweet petunia that I would be coming in behind him hanging on for dear life. I loved the freedom that I felt on the back of the bike, an excitement stirred inside me, I was on a real high as I rode in on a Harley at three different weddings. One was at a farm a few miles north of Balgonie a town one-half hour from Regina. It felt wonderful with the wind blowing through my three hair and a big biker teddy bear to hang onto as we were going down the highway.

The second one was a short ride at Craven campground where I came in behind the groom on a motorcycle and the bride came in on a golf cart. I had to fold up my robe to be sure that it wouldn't get caught on anything. Knowing my luck, something would go astray, and we would roll the bike before we got to the front of the venue. As far as Bob was concerned, his biking days were over. He shook his head at the first request but did not object. When I rode in for a third time Bob said, "Edna, do what you want." It became second nature, but it was always a thrill for me. The third time was at Truly Unique Country Weddings. What captivated me about this moment was the majestic beauty of the landscape of this space. I loved being whisked through the colorful flower beds and the beautiful shrubbery and trees. Having the beauty of nature all around me and being on the back of a motorcycle culminated into great excitement and a truly unique and unforgettable experience for me.

I often wondered what has happened to the couples I married. Below is the story of the biker wedding of Mike and Bonnie Atchinson and their life thereafter. Mike is the son of a popular Saskatchewan Roughrider football player, Ron Atchinson. I asked them to tell me their story right from when they met and what happened to their lives after the wedding day.

They met at a biker fundraiser for prostate cancer called, "Who's Your Daddy?" Mutual friends introduced them that night. The next morning a bunch of them went for breakfast and a group ride on motorcycles, and since that day they have been pretty much inseparable. Mike proposed to Bonnie at the German Club in exactly the same spot where they first met and decided to get married.

That is a lot more romantic than Bob proposing to me in the car in front of our house. In daylight, yet. But I just closed my eyes and imagined that we were someplace romantic in the dark. I was so excited and elated to receive a beautiful sparkling diamond ring and immediately said, "YES." Bob had to leave for work, so I ran up and down the street and showed all the neighbours my new engagement ring.

Mike and Bonnie had an outside wedding at Truly Unique Country Weddings. The owner had a sign put up called Biker Boulevard for the bikes to park. On the way to the rehearsal, their best man crashed his bike and broke his collar bone on the fresh gravel that was on the road. They had to get a replacement friend to stand in for him. The next day at the wedding it was a stifling hot one as it was 38 degrees of pure heat and no breeze. I rode in on the back of the Groom's nice blue Ultra-Harley. The bride wore a black lace floor-length wedding dress that made it feel even hotter that afternoon. Her son that was standing up in the wedding party ended up passing out, and a few other people had to be taken into the house on the property to be in the air conditioning as they felt faint as well.

Two days later they were set to go on their honeymoon, but it was pouring rain and Mike opted to take his bike as was planned and Bonnie did not feel comfortable doing that, so she followed behind with the car. Mike felt since they had all the campgrounds booked already, he didn't want to lose their deposits. A friend that was to come with them on his motorcycle was a retired motorcycle RCMP officer and he chose to meet up with them after the rain let up. They started out to B.C.

Suddenly they hit a bad rainstorm and Mike lost control of his bike due to hydroplaning. He ended up flipping his bike a couple of times and rolling down the highway landing on his head five times fracturing his wrist, broken ribs, and suffered some brain damage. They spent their honeymoon in the hospital for six days. Due to my frequent falls, I can certainly relate to Mike's broken bones, fractured ribs and wrists, and smashed elbow. Luckily, no brain damage.

A couple of years later Mike was coming home from Moose Jaw from a contract job that had ended for the workers, and they would be coming back to that job site two weeks later to finish. Bonnie received a call from Mike saying he was calling on someone's phone and he had just rolled his truck on a gravel road. Bonnie couldn't believe it. She left work and went to where he was laying in an ambulance and there wasn't much left of his truck, and it was still on its side. She met him at the hospital. At this point they were starting to know the hospital staff.

Bonnie often wonders how one person has this much bad luck. His Dr. suggested not to ride anymore and to walk around in a big bubble because he was an accident-prone train wreck. Bob often said after one of my many accidents that he should keep me barefoot and pregnant to keep me safe. Mike decided to sell his Harley and rather not ride but have a happy life with his hot wife. Mike will miss the long trips with Bonnie on the back of the bike, but it is so much more relaxing in a nice SUV or truck.

Now they have been accident-free for the longest period of time, knock on wood, and through all of this Bonnie couldn't imagine going through this with anyone else. Like Mike, I have had my share of tumbles, falls and accidents and I am so grateful that I had Bob by my side through all of it.

The groom (Mike) escorting Edna to the front of the venue on a Harley.

LADY FATHER

Edna loves motorbikes.

Bride and groom, Bonnie and Mike.

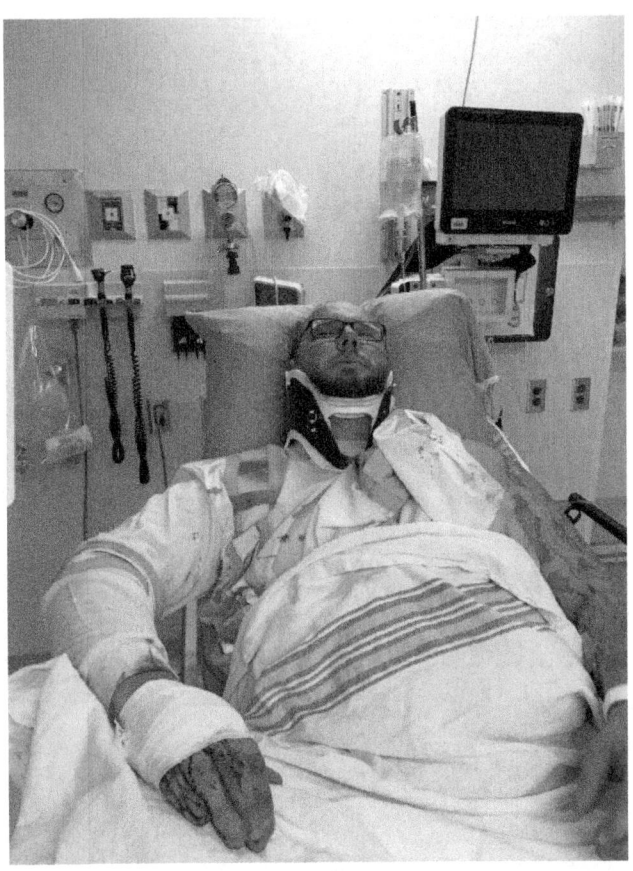

The start of Bonnie and Mike's honeymoon.

CHAPTER 13: CRASHES AND FALLS

It was January 7, and unbeknownst to us, it had rained during the night and froze. There was a sheet of ice everywhere. My husband took the truck and went to meet his buddies for coffee. I took the Mercury Marquis and headed downtown to my hairdresser.

I soon found out how icy the conditions were. I was going at a slower speed. Down Lewvan Drive. The light had turned yellow and the three cars in front of me went through the light as it turned red, I decided I couldn't make it and stopped suddenly. Since this vehicle was a rear-wheel drive I spun around and took down the centre light standard on Lewvan Drive and 4th Avenue. The whole side of my car was damaged, the window smashed, and glass hit my head, face, and shoulders. Luckily, I had glasses on. I hit a car in the oncoming lane, turned right, and continued to drive for two blocks against the traffic. It finally dawned on me I had to stop. I was in total shock. I was not injured, at least I didn't feel anything then.

It wasn't long before the police arrived and determined that my vehicle was not drivable. They called a tow truck and stayed with me until the tow truck came and towed it to SGI. I was so worried that Bob would be coming home from coffee and see his car smashed and being towed. Fortunately, he didn't.

The kind policeman offered me a ride home. I said, "No, I can't go home." He asked why, and I responded with, "I have to go to the hairdresser. I have two weddings to do this afternoon." He looked at me in amazement and said, "Okay, if that's where you want to go, I will take you there." He delivered me to the Hair Dressing Shop downtown.

In the meantime, of all the years that I have gone to the Hairdresser, I have never been late. After fifteen minutes and appearing to be a no-show they became concerned and called my house – there was no answer. They tried a few more times. They became concerned that something had happened. Finally, I arrived at the shop and as I went in, I became emotional.

They had to practically turn me upside down to get all the shards of glass out of my hair and head, on my face, and all over my coat. They did my hair and then now to phone Bob. This is the vehicle that he was most proud of out of twenty-one vehicles that he had owned in his lifetime. Of course, again, I start bawling like a drama queen. Bob could hardly understand what I was saying and was concerned that I was hurt. My husband, as usual, was a gem about the whole incident and wished that he had driven me instead.

Once again, I pulled myself together as I did not want to disappoint the couples. If I said I was going to be there then I wanted to be there. I went and did the weddings that day. The one and only time that I had to cancel was when Bob was ill and was in palliative care. I was not going to leave his side.

The day after my accident, a huge Bridal Fair was on at the Centre of the Arts. I was asked to be the guest speaker on behalf of all the marriage commissioners. I went to the Bridal Fair, did my speaking engagement, and came home feeling fine. That night I had nightmares and couldn't sleep, I totally fell apart. Delayed reaction. I was happy I was able to hold it together until I was done with what I had to do in those two days. I was a busy person with things to do every day. Bob had to drive me to all these events and pick me up. My water exercises twice a week, RCMP Depot scenario acting, and volunteering at the Floral Conservatory.

Bob was finally fed up with driving me everywhere I had to go. He said, "I thought we were retired?" "I think it's time we bought you your own car so you can drive yourself wherever you want to go." Bob was more used to a slower pace. The next day we went car shopping, and I hated every vehicle I saw. We came home with no car.

The transportation duties for Bob continued for two more weeks. Looking back, I believe I was traumatized from the accident. I started feeling better and more confident and felt that I could now look at vehicles and perhaps even drive one.

We went looking and found one that was an all-wheel drive and much safer for me. The salesman took us for a drive and stopped the car, got out and said, "Mrs. McCall take the wheel." I said, "I can't, Bob can." He said, "No, Bob has his truck you will be driving the car."

I hesitantly got in behind the wheel and drove. I couldn't believe how calm and confident I was. The salesman said, "You drive it home for the weekend and decide if this is the car you would like." I did, and we purchased it. It was not a Mercury Marquis, and we never did buy another one, however, we got to love the Ford Fusion. Over the years there would be an odd comment about the Mercury Marquis. Bob would draw my attention by saying, "Oh, there goes a Mercury Marquis." I knew how much that car meant to him, and I truly felt bad for what had happened. Those would be my silent moments.

Anyone who knows me knows that I have a history of falling, breaking bones, spraining my wrist, getting black eyes, wearing a cast or a brace, and using crutches. You can say that I am accident-prone. This incident was the mother of them all. We were having a rehearsal at Regina

Inn/Double Tree with a large wedding party. There was a riser about two feet high, large enough to accommodate the complete wedding party, and the signing table was situated at one end of the stage. The rehearsal was almost finished when I went over to the signing table which was at the edge of the stage. As I turned, I fell backward off the riser. Everyone rushed over to see how badly hurt I was, as I was in excruciating pain. Bob was sick with worry knowing that it was bad since I have a high tolerance for pain. The ambulance was called, and I was immediately transported to the General Hospital. I will never forget that ride. It was so, so, rough and I hurt so badly. I remember telling the ambulance driver, "You are so good-looking but a hell of a poor driver." I can't remember if he even was that good-looking. It wasn't his driving at all, it was that I was in so much pain. The Dr. on call determined from the x-rays that I did not have any fractures. I thought, *Okay, I can do the weddings the next day.*

But oh, I hurt so badly. Fortunately, I was able to go home by midnight. When we got into the house shortly after midnight, the phone was ringing. It was the bride who was upset as she was unsure if I was going to be able to do their ceremony. I said, "Yes, I will be there come hell or high water."

The next morning things were not getting better, I couldn't walk because I was in so much pain. We determined that the only way I could do the wedding was to do it in a wheelchair. Bob went out and got one for me. The best man offered to wheel me up to the front. As I was being wheeled down the aisle, I heard the oohs and awes. The guests that knew me were shocked to see me in a wheelchair. I began my opening remarks with, "I tried flying last night and it didn't quite work out." They burst out laughing which broke the tension in the room but did not relieve my pain. I managed to put my pain on the back burner and place my focus on the ceremony. This was important to do not only for this couple because I had another couple waiting for me to do their ceremony right after this one.

A couple of days later, after another set of x-rays, I found out that I, in fact, had five fractured ribs. The swelling was so bad they couldn't tell from the first set of x-rays. This is not the last that you will hear of my falls and fractures.

Edna did not fall alone this time.

Smashed elbow cast in disguise.

Another Fall in Orange Shoes

I had just purchased a new pair of orange shoes trimmed with gold. I was so proud to be wearing them for the first time to a wedding at the Conexus Art Centre. That was the only accessory the guests could see beside my robe. There were quite a few people in attendance.

As I proceeded down the long aisle with my portfolio in hand, I tripped on the rug and landed on the floor. I quickly picked myself up and proceeded to gather my portfolio while a young fellow in the aisle seat scrambled to assist me with picking up my marriage documents. I walked to the front turned to face the audience, pretended to brush myself off much to their laughter, and walked over picked up the mic, and came back to the centre and said, "Please rise." Thus, the groom entered leading the procession and the ceremony started.

CHAPTER 14:
THE DARNDEST PLACES

A Chaplin at the Regina Correctional Centre usually performed the civil ceremony; however, they did not have a Chaplin for a while. During this time, I did several marriage ceremonies at the Regina Correctional Centre.

Since my husband came with me to all my weddings, I had no problem going out there. He was often the witness. He and I both had clearance and would be referred by the other marriage commissioners. They were mostly women who didn't feel comfortable going to the Correctional Centre by themselves.

The Security Guard would bring the groom into a large room where guests would normally visit. The bride was already there. We would stay a distance away to give them their privacy prior to the ceremony. Sometimes we would even pick up the bride and give her a ride out.

This one day we had just arrived to do a ceremony when there was an all-out alert that an inmate had escaped. We had to wait until they caught him before we could proceed to marry the couple two hours later.

I would like to expand on one ceremony that I can vividly remember to this day. As we entered the Correctional Centre, we got clearance and proceeded to the waiting room, the bride was already there. If she wasn't in her sixties then she certainly looked like she was, you could tell she had a rough life. She had a huge family bible that she was holding with some artificial flowers on top. Shortly after, a sharp-looking young man came in and walked directly to her. He was in his mid-twenties and was incarcerated for one more year. We introduced ourselves and after a short discussion, we proceeded with the ceremony. After the ceremony was over he wanted to make sure that he was able to change his surname to hers. He was quite concerned that this should happen. In fact, he wanted her surname written on the marriage certificate instead of his surname. I had to do some tall-talking to convince him that he could use her surname however, it would not be on the marriage certificate.

The groom being a greenskeeper at a golf course saw no better place than to get married on the ninth hole of the golf course. The golfers were stopped on the eighth hole much to their chagrin until the ceremony was over. No one could wear heels on the greens. If they had heels they had to take their shoes off. There were about thirty guests at the ceremony standing around the ninth hole greens. After the ceremony, the couple drove away in a golf cart decorated with balloons to a barbeque reception.

Rocking the Valley was a huge annual musical festival held out in a valley half an hour outside of Regina. I was excited when I found that the couple wanted to get married at the festival. As we entered the grounds of Rocking the Valley, the gatekeeper asked us where our spot was. As we did not have tickets to attend the festival, I had to tell him we were going to site B44 to perform a marriage ceremony there. They knew about the wedding and were expecting us and immediately escorted us to the site. The couple, Doug and Cindy were fans of the festival and they decided to get married there.

At 1:00 p.m. July 12, 2003, there were twenty-four friends and family at the ceremony and 30,000 guests at the reception. I helped the bride get dressed since she had difficulty finding her underwear she was so nervous.

During the ceremony I could feel their happiness as they looked at each other while saying their vows. Their children all met for the first time.

After the ceremony the organizers had them on stage and gave them $75.00 worth of drink tokens and the party began. Then Cindy got to throw her bouquet off the stage in the Beer Gardens. The next day the media arrived and interviewed them, their interview was featured in the Regina Leader Post and Saskatoon Star Phoenix.

The couple honeymooned in Africa two weeks later with his brother Richard who lives gave them the trip as a wedding gift. Richard and Doug were separated by adoption as infants, this was the first time they met. They had three weeks to catch up on a lifetime of memories.

Over the years they relocated to Fort Qu'Appelle and have attended The Craven Jamboree every year since 2003. Ten years later I got a call from Doug asking me to perform their vow renewal in the same spot. Which I did. I reached out to Doug and Cindy recently and asked her if she still gets shivers when they kiss. She replied a simple, "yes," and laughed.

Rockin the Valley Wedding (Doug and Cindy).

One day while looking through the community flyer I saw a class to register for belly dancing. In my excitement, I immediately signed up because it sounded like a lot of fun, and I needed something to fill my evenings. I didn't ask, nor did I mention this idea to any of my family or friends because they would think I was crazy and had lost my mind. But I was pumped and eager to attend my first class. My instructor was born in the UK and her husband was born in Regina. They had a destination wedding. Because three countries were involved they were struggling to get their legal marriage certificate. It was becoming quite costly. We got talking about me being a marriage commissioner. She was tired of not being able to get her marriage certificate without a substantial cost and the length of time it was taking. I said to her, "All you need to do is get a marriage license and book me and we will get it done." She was so happy that it was so simple and so quick. They wanted to start a family, but they wanted to be legally married.

They arranged for me to perform their marriage ceremony in their Tattoo Parlor that the groom owned. They closed for the afternoon and decorated it. There were approximately twenty invited guests in attendance. To me, it felt like any other venue. To this day I am sorry I didn't exchange my fee for a tattoo.

I answered another advertisement that was looking for volunteer actors for cadet training at the RCMP Depot. This turned my crank. It was exactly what I was looking for to express my love for acting, taking the stage, and performing in front of an audience. In the beginning, the criteria were simpler however, it wasn't long before I was approached to do the cadets' final exams. This required me to follow the criteria explicitly and to be sure I delivered a high-level performance as the outcomes of these exams were pass or fail. It was after one of these days that I came home from the RCMP Depot. I was giddy with excitement and anxious to tell my husband Bob all about my scenario as a drunk driver. This scenario was the cadet's final exam.

The scenario was a drunk driver. I was given the criteria and an unmarked police car which I drove acting like a drunk around the perimeter at Depot. The cadet was following me in a police car with the instructor beside him. A delivery truck was coming toward me and I proceeded to turn into his lane and quickly swerved out again. I did that a couple of times scaring the driver of the delivery truck I'm sure, and the cadet. He immediately put the siren on, and I took my time in stopping, swerving a few more times until I slowly came to a stop. The daredevil in me was loving every moment of this.

The cadet asked me to turn the window down and

asked me my name. I deliberately hesitated to give my name and I told the young cadet that I had forgotten my name because I had so many of them. I could tell that he was under great stress as he was anxious to pass his final exam. I was determined to make him work for it. He then opened the door and asked me to get out several times. I placed my foot at the front inside of the vehicle and pretended to try to get out. I acted as though my leg wouldn't move without help so I drunkenly said, "I'm shtuck." After asking me a few more times to get out, he grabbed my leg rather aggressively and pulled it out of the car. He told me to get out. As I wobbled back and forth, leaning against the vehicle, he started the search. He asked me to open my jacket so he could pad me down. I said to him "keepsh goin that feels sho good." Glancing over at the Sergeant, he was having a hard time keeping a straight face which only encouraged me to amp it up. I thought I better cool my jets as I noticed the cadet was getting frustrated and nervous. I was happy to hear that the cadet passed his rigorous exam. When it was over the Sergeant said to me, "If your hair and lipstick weren't perfect, I would say that you were drunk. Great job." I was happy to hear that I passed as well.

When I arrived back home after my Golden Globe performance, Bob had my wine poured for our four o'clock happy hour. While we were sitting in our office I said to Bob, "I was a drunk driver again today." Bob always looked forward to hearing about my episodes. He would often laugh and shake his head at the shenanigans I pulled. He was a great audience for me to share my events of the day. I was telling the story with my usual excitement and giddiness when the phone rang. I answered with a pleasant, "Hello." The voice at the other end said, "Hello, this is Rob from Wolf 104.9 – our local radio station – I immediately thought that he might be wanting some information regarding the Floral Conservatory. This is not what he wanted. What he said was, "I would like to ask you if you would be willing to do a wedding at a wrestling match." I was still feeling giddy, so without hesitation, I laughingly said, "Sure." He repeated the request several more times to which I always said, "Sure," and giggled each time – I was not comprehending the magnitude of his request. Finally, he caught on that what I was saying was that I would do it, so he gave me a few details about the event. He said that it was going to be a sanctioned WWE wrestling match.

There would be a lot of people in attendance, and it will be held at the Agridome. The ceremony would be performed in the wrestling ring just prior to the wrestling match. What I did not know, was that he had asked my friend Elizabeth if she would do the wedding, and she had declined because she was just recuperating from a broken leg. She told him to, "Ask Edna McCall, and don't take no for an answer until she agrees to do it. She is probably the only one that will do it and she will do a darn good job."

Therefore, Rob was trying to talk me into it all along until he realized that I was agreeing to do it. As Bob was listening to what just happened, always the methodical one, he started asking questions about different situations and how was I going to deal with them. I became apprehensive and worried. However, I decided that I had made a promise and I would go through with it come what may.

As we started working together in preparation for the big day, I was advised that one woman volunteered to get married who worked at Wolf 104.9. There had been a contest to select another couple, therefore it would be a double ceremony. The wedding was an added incentive for advertising the event.

To entice couples to enter the contest, they were provided a wedding dress for up to $750.00. Tuxedo rental, rings (gold band), bouquets of flowers, boutonnieres, limo service, hotel rooms, and a wedding cake.

I arranged a meeting with both couples. I had one couple come half an hour earlier to do the personal statistical information, and then I had the other couple join us with the four of them on how we would proceed with the ceremony including their ideas.

It was decided that each would pick a different marriage vow, and each would pick a different ring vow from the choices I had. The first couple left, and I continued the interview with their personal information with the second couple.

The rehearsal was set for the afternoon prior to the wrestling match. The rehearsal lasted two and a half hours with most of the time being spent on where the wrestler's territory was by their security team, and where the wedding party was allowed to walk by the Agridome's security team. The WWE Security did not want anyone crossing over their territory and the Agridome's security was not happy with those decisions. It took the better part of two hours to get all that sorted out. It was ridiculous.

The next day finally arrived with much trepidation on my part. My ulcer was quirking.

There were 7000 people in attendance. The Agridome was full since it was such a huge event. I mean huge the likes of Hulk Hogan and other big names including women wrestlers who were on tour through Western Canada. Two of my grandsons, Derrick and Kelly, were in attendance.

Let's get ready to ruuummmmbblllleeee! I was ushered into the wrestling ring by two wrestlers, a man named Sand Storm from Calgary and a woman we will call Miss Louisiana who were the witnesses for both couples. There was the booing and the cheering at the same time. I immediately knew they were not booing or cheering for me since they did not know me. I found out later that it was Sand Storm they were cheering for since he was their hometown boy, and the booing was for Miss Louisiana since she was an aggressive, feisty wrestler. As I was standing there overlooking the crowd of over 7000 people, I had a feeling of great anxiety, nervousness, and apprehension. I thought to myself, "Can I pull this off?" "Will I pass out?" Will I screw this up?" To top it all off, I had never done a double ceremony before either.

There was no elegant way of entering the ring. One of the brides wore a high-neck wedding dress and the other wore a revealing dress. My grandson Derrick proceeded to tell his mom that one of the bride's dresses was so low that you could see what she ate for breakfast. Finally, the moment arrived, and I began the ceremony with "we are gathered here today," the crowd went, "Wha-a-a-t," thankfully, one of the grooms was in communications and warned me about this prior to the ceremony. In previous matches, there was a wrestler that whenever someone spoke to him, he would say, "Wha-a-a-t," ultimately the crowd caught on to this. He suggested I give them their moment of fame and continue. With that in mind, I decided to make my remarks brief since this was a wrestling crowd and not a wedding crowd. Wha-a-at happened a few more times. Derrick was bothered by this and I was touched to learn that after the wrestling match he said to his mother, "Mommy, the people were sure mean to Gramma." Why do you say that she asked, "Because they would not let her talk, they kept saying, 'Wha-a- t.'" She replied, "Grandma would not have done it if she was thin-skinned."

However, they did respect the couples when they said their vows. When the first couple completed their vows, they went back and tagged the second couple to come forward for their vows. (As in a tag team match) to my surprise.

I saw Pat Fiacco, Mayor of Regina, sitting not far from the ring. It was a bit daunting I might say. The fathers of the brides were not exactly beaming with happiness to see their daughters getting married in a wrestling ring. Added to that, the crowd was not into a wedding with couples kissing. They bought tickets for a wrestling match, and they wanted to see the likes of Hulk Hogan and other top-named wrestlers get into action. The crowd was happy to have the ceremony over with and so was I. I followed the couples out of the ring. I was elated to have gotten through without fainting, fumbling, or falling. After the ceremony, we were invited to the Box Office for the cutting of the cake. I thanked them much and told them that I had another commitment. When we got home Bob immediately poured me a glass of wine to relax from the most daunting experience that I have ever had in performing a marriage ceremony, without a doubt.

In the ring.

Country Wedding

I always love going to the country weddings since they put so much work into making their yards so gorgeous.

Since I am a gardener I especially enjoy and appreciate the work that goes into this to make it so beautiful. It was a hot day, +36C, the wedding was at 5:00 p.m. in the east end of the yard where there was some shade. I performed the ceremony with laryngitis, thank goodness for a microphone the guests were able to understand what I was saying. The bride and groom each had five attendants. The ceremony was enjoyed by about 100 people. What made it even more special was the optional letter and wine box ceremony they chose.

At the appropriate time, I shared these words with Eric and Bailey to solidify their letter and wine box ceremony,

"Like good wine, a great love will deepen and mature with age. This box contains a bottle of wine and a love letter from each to the other. The letters describe the good qualities they find in one another, the reasons they fell in love and their reasons for choosing to marry. The letters are sealed in individual envelopes, and they have not seen what the other has written. Eric and Bailey, you have created your own romantic time capsule to be opened on your tenth wedding anniversary. I recommend that you keep the box in a place of honor prominently displayed in your home as a constant reminder of your commitment to each other. Eric and Bailey should you ever find your marriage enduring insurmountable hardships, you are to as a couple, open this box, sit, and drink the wine together, then separate and read the letters you wrote to one another when you were united as a couple in marriage. By reading these love letters you will reflect upon the reasons you fell in love and chose to marry each other here today. The hope is, however, that you will never have a reason to open this box. And if this is the case, you are to open this box to share and enjoy on your tenth-year wedding anniversary. Eric and Bailey, you may now seal the box."

For the couples to have the option to customize the ceremony in a way that resonates with their heart and feelings is what makes me love performing marriage ceremonies and makes it so much more special.

Eric and Bailey share their love at sunset.

CHAPTER 15:
WEDDING PARTY BLOOPERS

You never know what to expect from a wedding party with the varied personalities and their behaviours. Some have fainted, some have cried, some have been complete jerks, and some have been angels. I have felt more like a ringmaster at a circus than a marriage commissioner at times. Over time, I learned to be more authoritative to support the wishes of the couple, rather than be bossed around by an aggressive bridesmaid or a know-it-all groomsman. Some think that just because they have attended a few weddings in their day, they are now an expert on how things should proceed. Rehearsals are essential when the wedding party has two or more attendants, each with a ring bearer and flower girl. Often the bride and groom were more comfortable having a rehearsal even for a small wedding. I would accommodate their wishes.

At first, I had difficulties with someone in the wedding party wanting to run the rehearsal exactly like theirs was when they got married. Since we had dealt with the details of how the couple wanted their wedding to proceed at our meeting, I had to inject with letting them know it was not how the couple wanted it. Sometimes they would argue. Often the couple wanted me to handle the whole situation since either their bridesmaid or groomsmen were strong and they wouldn't be able to get what they wanted. I found out quickly to be firm with them and say, "This is the way the bride and groom would like to have it."

One groomsman would not take no for an answer, he said, "I have been to three weddings and have a damn good idea how things are done." I came back with, "I have performed 1,000 ceremonies and I know exactly how things are done – to the bride and groom's wishes – not yours, theirs. He sat down on the steps and pouted through the whole rehearsal.

I didn't always get the support required from the groomsmen and sometimes they would become the center of attention at the ceremony. A big burly type of guy, who was a best man, sobbed openly during the ceremony. I always have tissues in my portfolio for the bride and groom however, I had to hand him all of what I had. He was all tough on the outside but a soft teddy bear on the inside.

Another groomsman in a huge wedding party in beautiful Kiwanis Park on a hot day fainted during the ceremony. I wasn't sure if I should stop the ceremony and give him CPR or what to do. The other groomsmen took him off to the side under the shade of a tree and the groom whispered to me to proceed since he was a diabetic. No one got too excited since this had happened before. The ambulance was called advising them it was in the middle of a wedding ceremony. They arrived and silently took him away.

Further, to my note about being a jerk at a rehearsal, I missed a step off the deck and did a flyby toward a groomsman. Rather than trying to break my fall, he quickly stepped aside as I went ass over tea kettle into the rose bushes that surrounded the deck. As I was struggling to get up with scratches all over my arms and legs, he came over and offered me his hand and said, "You were coming so fast I thought you would take me down with you." I refused his hand and told him to get lost.

But I have also experienced groomsmen being angels in

disguise. They have asked me to take their arm and have assisted me in climbing over obstacles, like rocks and debris, climbing up unusually high and sometimes narrow steps, as well as complimenting me on how beautiful my service was. These groomsmen are like a box of chocolates, you never know what you are going to get.

And sometimes, ring bearers lose the precious cargo they are carrying. The wedding was at Kiwanis Waterfall Garden. The three-year-old had the rings tied to his satin pillow while walking through the park to be with the wedding party who had gathered at the opposite end of the park. When he arrived where the bride and bridesmaids were gathered, the rings were missing from his pillow. The tie had come undone.

The search started with the bridesmaids and the groomsmen all backtracking where the little fellow had walked. When they anticipated where the rings might be, the girls in their beautiful long dresses and high-heeled shoes got down on their knees searching in the grass. After some time had elapsed the groom was asked if we could proceed without the rings. He refused to start and insisted the rings must be found. The little fellow was so upset since he knew he had lost them.

My husband Bob would often stand back from the crowd and watch the comings and goings of the crowd. He was always looking into the crowd to see if there was anyone he knew. When there was a delay in the ceremony, he came over to me and asked me what was going on. I said to him that the ring bearer lost the rings, both the wedding bands and the diamond ring. He casually walked over to where the women were crawling around on their hands and knees feeling in the grass hoping to find the rings. Bob, with his eagle eyes, noticed something glistening a little distance from the girls. He walked over, picked up the rings out of the grass, and handed them to a relieved maid of honour. They all screamed for joy. Bob saved the day. I couldn't get to the groom fast enough to tell him the good news. The ring bearer was calmed down and was given the pillow with the rings tied in a double knot. The ceremony proceeded with a much-relieved bride and groom, wedding party, and of course, the marriage commissioner.

Rings being an intricate part of a wedding, I experienced a unique way for the guests to send their best wishes to the couple. As the wedding party proceeded down the aisle, the rings tied with raffia were sent throughout the guests. They had instructions to make good wishes for the couple and then pass them on. The rings arrived back up to the best man just in time for the ring ceremony. I was pleasantly surprised at how the rings arrived in perfect time for the ceremony. I took the rings now enhanced with all the good wishes from friends and family and proceeded with the ring ceremony.

It always delights me to see the flower girls dressed so eloquently in lace, ankle socks, and patent shoes, as well as their hair curled often with a big bow matching their dress. I performed a ceremony with two little darlings as flower girls. This wedding began with the piper piping the wedding procession into the Saskatchewan room at Hotel Saskatchewan. The bride and the maid of honour each had a little two-year-old that were two days apart. They each carried a sunflower and were dressed alike in A-line little navy-blue dresses. Halfway through the service, just before I started the vows, the maid of honour's little girl pulled her dress over her head and took it off. She was standing there in nothing but her diaper. I saw the look of horror on her grandma's face who was ready to leap to the rescue. When I looked and saw that the little flower girl had taken off her dress I said," She did that right on cue," to which everyone burst out into laughter. Grandma ran up and put the dress back on. Flower girls too, like to steal the show.

Making a lifetime commitment to spend the rest of your life with someone is a big decision. It's no wonder that sometimes people get cold feet. That happened to one particular groom who looked happy and was looking forward to getting married the night before at rehearsal. The next day at the wedding, everyone was on time including the bride. When asked where the groom was, the best man said he was coming on his own. He had not arrived. When they tried to contact him, he did not answer his phone. One-half hour went by and still no groom. I felt sorry for the bride. She looked so worried and upset. I had another wedding scheduled and needed to move on. I was contemplating leaving and mentioned to one of the parents that I could return after I was finished with the other ceremony. They asked if I could please stay for a few more minutes. I tried calling the groom myself, but he hung up on me. Then, I tried calling ahead to my next appointment to advise them that I was going to be late, but the groom had already turned off his cell phone in preparation for the ceremony. I learned a lesson from this. From that moment on, I tell the groom to keep his cell phone on until my arrival, and that has worked miraculously ever since.

Soon thereafter, the groom decided to show up and I started the ceremony immediately if not sooner. I abbreviated my ceremony and spoke a lot faster than I normally do in order to get to the other wedding that I was already late for. I am glad the groom thawed out his cold feet because my feet were on hot coals to get to my next appointment. Now Bob had to drive like a maniac. It was moments like this that Bob would say, "I need a bloody plane to get you from point a to point b."

I have had my run-ins with brides as well. There are brides who can be a gem to deal with and there are others that are stressed, and the diva begins to show through. And then there is the bride in a group of her own – the Bridezilla. That is when you just stand back out of her road and let her rip. It has to be her way or the highway. It started the day before at rehearsal. She was quite demanding. No one could make her happy. The chairs were not placed right, and various other things were misplaced and not to her liking. To top it off, after inviting 250 guests she delivered the whopper that she didn't want to be able to see the guests because it made her nervous, and she wanted the wedding held in total darkness. Silly me for telling her that I had a book light which meant there was no reason to have any lights on.

We proceeded with the ceremony in the dark hoping my batteries were not going to die. It was difficult as I struggled with my limited vision. The guests were complaining they couldn't see anything. I was unable to deliver my ceremony as smoothly as I could under normal circumstances, but I got the job done.

As I walked down the aisle the guests said, "Good job." In retrospect, I left wondering why she would invite 250 guests and not want them to see her walk down the aisle. Why not just come to my house or her house with witnesses only and get married? Perhaps she got nervous and anxious just like the groom who got cold feet. Regardless, I was happy to be on my way home.

While in the car Bob said to me, "Guess what I did tonight?" I replied, "What?"

Bob said, "I slipped in and sat at the first table by the door with all strangers. A woman at the table eventually asked, "Are you on the bride's side?" Bob said, "No," silence. A little while later she said, "Are you with the groom's side?" He said, "No," silence. Finally, she asked "Who do you know, the bride or the groom?" He said, "nobody," there was more silence. He then thought he better say something, "I was just walking by and saw there was a wedding going on, and there is always good food so I thought I would come in and have a good meal." They had shocked looks on their faces and more silence. Finally, he said, "My wife is the marriage commissioner."

That was so out of character for him. I just couldn't believe that he would do that with strangers. As I mentioned before, he is an introvert and would not open up to strangers unless they spoke first. When I told our kids, they too, could not believe that Dad would do that and kidded him a lot about it. Once again, Bob poured me a glass of wine and himself a vodka to end the day.

Throughout my career, I have had to work with wedding planners. Some good and some not so great. At this one particular wedding which was at the beginning of my career, the wedding planner decided that the wedding party should be on the stage facing the audience, and I was to stay on the main floor facing the wedding party which was some distance away with my back toward the audience.

There were three videographers. As each one entered the hall they took their places. The first videographer to the left asked me not to stand so that I would be in his way. The second videographer claimed his spot to the right and asked me not to stand where I would block his view. The third videographer in the centre asked me to be sure not to stand in the centre since he wanted the full view of the wedding party.

I became so frustrated with all of that including the wedding planners' instructions. The time had come to start, and I was trying to be conscious as to where I was standing while I was seething with anger. I felt uncomfortable that the bride and groom were so far away from me. As the ceremony progressed the bride became emotional. I didn't know what to do to calm her down as I was too far away to hand her a tissue or to quietly ask her to take a deep breath. I did feel like crawling onto the stage, however, I silently waited for her to get control. It was embarrassing for the bride as well since she was facing the audience.

After the ceremony on my way out, I had so many compliments on what a fantastic job I had done. I thought, *Wow, I must perform well under stress, pressure, and being pissed off.*

CHAPTER 16:
HOW I BECAME LADY FATHER

Not everyone who gets married stays together. I always hope that when I unite two people that their commitment to each other lasts a lifetime. However, I understand this is not always the case, and sometimes couples choose to divorce for various reasons. One couple that I got to know, had been married for fourteen years and had four children, and then divorced. He proceeded to marry someone else but after six years they divorced as well. Interestingly enough, the groom then came back to his first wife. I married the couple on September 6, 1996. They have nine grandchildren who were thrilled and giggled to see grandpa and gramma kissing. They were touched by the service since they thought that all the groom originally wanted was to say the vows and sign the documents. They lived together for sixteen years. At the meeting, I asked them why they chose to get remarried, and the groom said, "The neighbors are starting to talk."

Sometimes I am asked to undo what I have already done. A 6-foot 6 inch popular football player for the Saskatchewan Roughriders came to my house with his fiancé for their meeting, along with their extremely cute little one-year-old boy. He was so happy to walk into my house because I had a high ceiling which meant he wouldn't have to duck upon entering. When asked what smaller venue they could use, I recommended The Floral Conservatory where they did end up choosing to marry. After the ceremony when the photo op was almost over, he came looking for me and asked, "Don't you want to have a picture with just you and me?" I said, "Sure, okay," and a picture was taken of just the two of us. What a diva. I guess he was used to people making such a fuss over him and wanting pictures with him all the time.

Three days after the wedding, I received a desperate call from an upset bride sobbing, asking me to annul their marriage. I said, "I can put you together, but I can't take you apart." We spoke for some time until she was calmed down and thought things over. She apologized to have bothered me. Last I heard they were still together.

However, I performed a marriage ceremony for a couple who were married for nine years and had three children. Ultimately they did divorce. A couple of years later I performed the ceremony for the groom who was marrying a different partner. A while later I performed the ceremony for the bride who also married a different partner. It was quite cute when I heard the son say to his mom, "Mommy, Mommy, that's the same lady who married Daddy." I had to laugh. Some people are superstitious and will not get the same marriage commissioner the second time around if their marriage didn't last. Obviously, this couple did not subscribe to this superstition which was good for my business.

Our friends were visiting us from Nashville, Tennessee. One evening we decided to go for a walk. We came upon several show homes and decided to go in and look around. When we entered one of the show homes, the Marketing Representative said to me, "I know you, you married us a couple of years ago." This often happens that I run into couples that I have married. It always interests me to see how they are doing, if they have started their family, and what they are doing as far as work. I have a number of couples that I have stayed in touch with over many years, and in fact, have become good friends with many of them. After hearing this woman say that I had married them, our friend Mike asked her, "Are you still married?" She said, "No," I immediately replied, "Don't blame me, I was not in their bedroom."

Someone did end up in the bedroom of one of the grooms that I was meant to marry. The bride called me a week before they were due to be married and canceled the wedding. This gave me the weekend off, or so I thought.

Not long after that call, I received another call from a fellow who worked with my husband as a bus operator. He said, "Hey, Lady Father, this is Gabe Dreher, are you available to perform a wedding next Saturday at 3:00 p.m.?" I laughed since I had not heard that terminology before. I said, "I just happened to have a cancellation for that time and date."

He proceeded to tell me about the young couple's dilemma. The young couple was getting married in the Catholic Church. The groom was Catholic, and the bride was divorced and Lutheran and they had one child together. The priest was there for a long time and knew them well. He told the couple that he did not always go by the book, but that he went by his conscience and he would marry them. Unfortunately, he died three weeks prior to the wedding.

When the couple met with the new priest to make preparations for their wedding, the priest informed them that he could not marry them since he goes by the book.

The groom's father was so devastated and told Gabe that the new priest would not marry the kids, "What are we going to do with 300 invited guests and less than two weeks before the wedding? How do you let 300 guests know that the wedding is changed to another place?" Gabe told him not to worry, that he had someone in mind who was the perfect person for the job. That is when I got the call. After I had indicated to him that I was available to do the wedding, the couple reached out and we immediately proceeded with the process as the wedding was less than two weeks away.

They got permission from the bishop for the couple to be married in the Catholic Church by a female marriage commissioner. I was in awe of the thought that I would be doing a wedding in the Catholic Church. I could not fathom it for a moment. However, I soon found out it was no different than any other venue. It was the people that could not accept the fact that a marriage commissioner and not a priest performed the marriage ceremony.

The priest, who had refused to do the couple's wedding, had a rehearsal just before mine the evening before. He was helpful in letting me know where the microphone was and how to use it and walked me through the church to familiarize me with this place.

The groom was upset he said, "Why are you letting the priest run your show, this is not his wedding, this is your wedding," I advised him that he was not interfering with my wedding, he was just showing me where everything was.

The next day the church was packed. The parishioners suddenly realized that the priest was not going to be doing the wedding since I was making preparation to set up at the front of the church with my robe on. There was much whispering going on.

As I was waiting in the lobby for the bride and her party to arrive, a lady came out of the sanctuary and asked me "What are you doing here?" I responded, "I am waiting for the bride to arrive, oh, here she comes," and walked away. What she meant was, why was I doing the wedding?

I performed the ceremony as I had in any other venue, however, this one had a bit of a twist, I knew that I had to shine to prove to the Catholic parishioners that a marriage commissioner was just as capable of delivering a heartfelt message as a priest even without the traditional Catholic tradition of including the mass.

After we left the church and went to our vehicle, a lady

came running after us. When I turned down the window she asked, "How come you did the ceremony instead of the priest?" I said, "The couple asked me," and we drove away.

It was about a year later and we were at a social event when I met up with Gabe who had referred me to the couple whose ceremony I performed in the Catholic Church. He said, "Hi, Lady Father, how are you doing? You owe me one for referring you," I said, "Ok, I will buy you a drink." We went up to the bar and I asked for a double for this gentleman for services rendered. While I was walking away, the bartender asked Gabe what the services rendered were for? All of a sudden I heard the two of them laughing hysterically. I wondered what came out of his mouth this time since you never knew what he was going to say. Later that evening when I went back to the bar I asked the bartender, "What did he say that was so funny?" The bartender replied, I asked him what the services rendered were for? He said, "You were a prostitute." I was horror-struck. I haven't got even with him – yet.

CHAPTER 17:
TRULY UNIQUE

Truly Unique Country Weddings was conceived in 2004, when in August of that year, Kerry Keller had an angina attack. He was stressed from his electrical contracting business. While he was in the hospital he was trying to figure out what he could do for a new business that could have customers come to his acreage. After a little homework, he came up with the idea. His yard was well treed, and he had already started some landscaping. It took until 2006 to finish and be open for customers. I was the first marriage commissioner hired by the first couple. Kerry and I were introduced before the rehearsal. We got along great right away. Kerry hired me for his 2007 open house where they put on a skit of a mock wedding. While the couples and guests were mingling there were some actors who scened a proposal spontaneously and decided to get married right then and there. Kerry yelled out to the crowd, "Is there a preacher in the house?" On cue I came forward, I was wearing my robe (a house-coat) there were a number of wedding specialists available for the open house. One of them had used wedding dresses and all of the things like bouquets and even an arbor were used. The couple went to the changing room in the walk-out basement and within twenty minutes there was a wedding. Of the fifty or so people that were there. I would say half were in disbelief that it was going on. I put on a good show with a little humour, that was a fun day. I have had a lot of practice acting.

One of the events stood out in Kerry's mind from the beginning. He had come up with the idea that all couples that got married at his place should have a little something that would make them cherish their day and remember his facility. His idea was that their names should be written in stone. Also, that the stone should stay in the path in the garden at the facility. It caught on right away after making the first one and presenting it to the couple in front of all to see. After the first wedding was over, there was a CD left behind with the couple's wedding music on it. One of the songs was called, *Written in Stone* by Randy Travis. As he listened to the words, he knew he could use this song to present the stone to the couples as the song was playing. That became the chosen song and the couples loved it.

It was about the sixth wedding that Kerry did the stone presentation, per usual. He didn't notice anything different about the stone, it was slate like the rest of them, maybe a little lighter than the rest. It wasn't until 2007 the following spring, that he saw a problem. A good size piece of a corner of the stone broke away. It hadn't affected the writing on it, but he was devastated. He had the belief that the marriage was written in stone, now it was broken.

He went to town the next day and went to the granite shop and bought the best epoxy he could find. He fixed the stone where there was a hairline crack where the frost had pushed it apart – that was a lesson. Later that same year, the couple returned to the venue for a cousin's wedding, as it turned out the couple had separated. He was freaked out, but never said anything about the stone. They were camped out at the venue in separate campers. Over the course of the weekend, he took the time to talk to each of them. The problem was that the groom wasn't ready to grow up yet, by his and her admission. Kerry said to both of them that the marriage was written in stone, and he had the proof in the path and they should give it another go. He chuckled to himself privately thinking, what would the odds be that a little pep talk might help. The next time he saw the woman was a couple of years later, it was in a grocery store in the city. She was pushing a baby carriage. Kerry was short on time and had no time to say hi and went on his way without her knowing he had seen her. Eleven years have now passed and 143 functions later, I performed the final ceremony for Kerry's friend's daughter's wedding.

On a weekend in mid-September 2016, Kerry had the final function. It was number 144 and was dedicated to all the couples who had gotten married there and the staff. A party with a few surprises, fireworks, free food, and camping was held. The bar was open. The first part of the day was the big deal, all who had a stone in the path could come and get theirs and take it home. After a couple of speeches, Kerry presented me with a stone of my own, "The McCall's" to take home. Over the course of the song, *Stairway to Heaven*, without rehearsal, every stone was lifted out of the pathway that extended some 180 meters of twisting garden edges and grass, by either couples or staff. Right down to the last note. It was wonderful. The last year of stones were made of granite and shaped like stairs. Later that day as Kerry was mingling with couples, many who were toting children, he came across the couple whose stone had broken. They now had two children and were happy. As they were talking, Kerry told them that he had something for them. He went to the shop and returned with a covered granite stone with their wedding date and names on it. They both looked at me puzzled. She asked what it was for. Kerry then told them the story of the broken one that they had now pulled from the ground. They informed me that the weekend they were there at their cousin's wedding was the start of the mending that was needed, and thanked Kerry for the encouragement. There may have been a tear shed there, I can't remember.

I was surprised and proud of my stone since I performed seventeen marriage ceremonies in this beautiful and unique venue over eleven years. Including the first wedding and the last wedding.

Edna being recognized for performing the most weddings at Truly Unique.

Truly Unique Country Weddings

CHAPTER 18:
TILL DEATH DO US PART

In conclusion, being a marriage commissioner has given my husband and me a busy and exciting life during our later years.

We would have had a much slower, quieter, life that would have driven me nuts. I am sure of this since I still had and have high energy. Our whole lifestyle changed. I would so look forward to meeting the couples to plan their ceremony. Bob would answer the door and greet them, and we would have a chat prior to the start of the meeting. There was a couple of times that I had double booked, and he would end up entertaining one couple while I had the meeting with the other couple. The weekends became our social life. We met so many lovely people as I've detailed and have become part of many families. By performing several weddings in one family dynamic, we became friends with these families.

Bob and I enjoyed getting to experience the different cultures be they ever so unique. We were always treated like royalty. What was so nice was that we would be invited to their cultural wedding the day prior to the wedding I was performing for them.

What is still great to this day is that I am in contact with quite a number of couples and have become friends with a lot of them. I have had the opportunity of meeting people of all ages from doctors to nurses, to lawyers to teachers, principals, office workers, tradespeople, and everything in between. The biggest lesson I learned was that people are unique and you have to go with the flow. You can give them options to allow them to make their choices and always make them feel that it is their idea.

I have enjoyed my retirement life so much because of my career as a marriage commissioner. If there is anything that I didn't like it was people constantly changing their minds after I have completed their paperwork. Every once in a while, I would get someone who was negative, and I tried hard to get them to see the world in a positive light. Sometimes I would even get a smile out of them. I know that my upbeat and personable attitude had a positive influence on the people that I met. I, in turn, developed great compassion for people as I learned about the obstacles that they had to overcome to be together. I never took a moment of this for granted.

I worked hard to give the best that I had so that couples could have the best experience possible. I would hope to be remembered for my sense of humour, my sincerity, my work ethic, my loyalty, and my spunky personality. The way that I live is to live life to the fullest.

Never so noticeable was Bob's love and caring when I became ill with Temporal Arthritis and lost vision in my right eye. There were three to four doctor appointments a week for the first year, and at least two a week for two years after that. In addition, I had weekly blood tests and had to see three different doctors sometimes waiting an hour and a half in the doctor's office. Never once did Bob complain, but many times he expressed his concern for my well-being.

In 2017 Bob's health deteriorated. In the final days, we were able to reminisce about our life together with both of us agreeing on having no regrets. Bob treated me like a princess, and I am forever grateful for his love, support, and dedication to me.

I continue to perform marriage ceremonies with the assistance of my daughters-in-law. I have since sold my house and I am a resident at the beautiful The Williston Retirement Community in Regina Saskatchewan.

ACKNOWLEDGMENTS

Thank you to my family for their love and support. To Liz who stepped in to drive me and assist me with rehearsals when Bob no longer could. Also to Rosanne who filled in when Liz was away. To my sons, Rod and Shawn, for their support during the last three years, which has meant so much to me.

To my two very dear friends, Bev Kirk and Marlene Pellerin, for their continuous curiosity on my progress, their support and encouragement.

Without my coach Denise Anderson, I would not have written this book and continued to only wish to write a book. I enjoyed the unique experience of how our energies complimented one another. So often we would have the same thought at the same time and even say the same words at the same time. Thank you for your encouragement and drive to make it happen.

To my editors, Cory and Hadley, it has been a great pleasure working with you both.

So, to the three of you – thank you for assisting me in bringing this book to print.

ABOUT THE AUTHOR

Edna I. McCall is an all-inclusive marriage commissioner who has performed more than 2,000 ceremonies for all cultures, ages, and sexual orientation since 1995. She has performed as many as seven weddings in one day, two of which being one-hour drives out of town since there were only six marriage commissioners for Regina and surrounding area at that time. From the very first wedding, she found herself emotionally involved with each couple she united. On occasion, she has asked several members of her family to act as witnesses and they, too, became emotionally bonded to these strangers.

Even in her professional role, Edna sometimes found it difficult to maintain her composure when two people were crying with joy and happiness directly in front of her.

She has performed marriages for prosecutors, lawyers, doctors, vice presidents, principals, teachers, same sex couples, Hindus, Muslims, Laos, Aboriginals, Philippines, Jewish, and many other cultures.

Edna grew up on a farm mixed with dairy and grain, acquiring a strong work ethic from a young age. She obtained her high school education and entered the work force in Regina. To improve her opportunities for promotion, Edna attended the University of Regina in the evenings to obtain a certificate in purchasing.

Upon retiring from a successful career in the work force after forty-five years and in addition to marrying people, she has devoted her life to volunteering at numerous events, occasions, and places, including acting. One of the places Edna volunteered at was The Regina Floral Conservatory for twenty years holding various executive positions. She was responsible for getting the name changed from, "The City of Regina Green House," to, "The Regina Floral Conservatory." Edna received a Lifetime Achievement Award for her contributions at the Conservatory.

Edna loves acting and has done so from when she was in school. She has been a scenario Actor for R.C.M.P. for ten years as well as acting in six shows for The Crimes of the Century on TV. She lives in Regina, Saskatchewan.

Made in the USA
Middletown, DE
06 September 2021